# Leading Your Team to Excellence

**The Corwin Press logo**—a raven striding across an open book—represents the happy union of courage and learning. We are a professional-level publisher of books and journals for K-12 educators, and we are committed to creating and providing resources that embody these qualities. Corwin's motto is "Success for All Learners."

# Leading Your Team to Excellence

## How to Make Quality Decisions

Elaine K. McEwan

CORWIN PRESS, INC.
A Sage Publications Company
Thousand Oaks, California

Copyright © 1997 by Corwin Press, Inc.

All rights reserved. The purchase of this copyright material confers the right on the purchaser to reproduce it by photocopying without specific authorization by the publisher.

*For information address:*

Corwin Press, Inc.
A Sage Publications Company
2455 Teller Road
Thousand Oaks, California 91320
e-mail: order@corwin.sagepub.com

SAGE Publications Ltd.
6 Bonhill Street
London EC2A 4PU
United Kingdom

SAGE Publications India Pvt. Ltd.
M-32 Market
Greater Kailash I
New Delhi 110 048 India

Printed in the United States of America

**Library of Congress Cataloging-in-Publication Data**

McEwan, Elaine K., 1941-
    Leading your team to excellence : how to make quality decisions / Elaine K. McEwan.
        p.  cm.
    Includes bibliographical references and index.
    ISBN 0-8039-6520-6 (alk. paper) — ISBN 0-8039-6521-4 (pbk. : alk. paper)
    1. School management and organization — United States — Decision-
making.   2. Decision-making, group.  I. Title.
LB2805.M24  1996
371.2'00973 — dc20                                      95-17300

This book is printed on acid-free paper.

    98  99  00  01  10  9  8  7  6  5  4  3  2

Corwin Press Production Editor: S. Marlene Head
Designed by Joan Gazdik Gillner
Production by Editorial Service and Publications Management
Cover Designer: Marcia R. Finlayson

ABOUT THE AUTHOR .................vii

INTRODUCTION .......................viii

# TABLE OF CONTENTS

■ CHAPTER ONE
## Understanding Decision Making: 1

| | |
|---|---|
| How do decisions actually get made? | 1 |
| What is quality decision making? | 4 |
| What are the advantages of team decision making? | 5 |
| What can go wrong with decision making? | 5 |
| When should decisions be made by a team? | 6 |
| What kinds of decisions should be made by a team? | 6 |
| What does a good team look like? | 7 |
| How can you conduct an effective meeting? | 9 |
| What is a group process? | 10 |
| How can you select a group process to meet your needs? | 11 |
| Are you ready to begin? | 11 |

■ CHAPTER TWO
## Group Processes for Building and Sharing Values: 13

| | |
|---|---|
| What is the importance of values in building a team that is capable of quality decisions? | 14 |
| What process activities can help my team to build and share values? | 15 |

■ CHAPTER THREE
## Group Processes for Building Teams: 33

| | |
|---|---|
| How does a group become a team? | 33 |
| What are the key factors that must be present for team development to take place? | 35 |
| What roles must be fulfilled on an effective team? | 35 |
| What are the early warning signals of team trouble? | 37 |
| What process activities can help build an effective team? | 38 |

■ CHAPTER FOUR
## Group Processes for Generating Ideas: 65

| | |
|---|---|
| What is creativity? | 65 |
| What can inhibit creativity? | 66 |
| What process activities can help my team generate quality ideas? | 67 |

## CHAPTER FIVE
# Group Processes for Sharing Critical Information: 81

| | |
|---|---:|
| How can I make sure my information is accurate and sufficient? | 81 |
| How do I know when the team has enough information to make a decision? | 82 |
| What are some ways to share research and information with my team? | 83 |

## CHAPTER SIX
# Group Processes for Problem Solving: 95

| | |
|---|---:|
| What kinds of problems are out there? | 96 |
| What are the characteristics of good problem solvers? | 97 |
| What are the seven steps to problem solving? | 97 |
| What process activities can promote productive problem solving? | 97 |

## CHAPTER SEVEN
# Group Processes for Reaching Consensus: 113

| | |
|---|---:|
| What is consensus? | 113 |
| What are some important guidelines/ground rules for consensus decision making? | 114 |
| Why is consensus so valuable for teams? | 115 |
| Is there a place for voting and ranking in the decision-making process? | 116 |
| What process activities can help promote consensus decision making? | 116 |

## CHAPTER EIGHT
# Group Processes for Resolving Conflict: 139

| | |
|---|---:|
| What is conflict resolution? | 139 |
| What kinds of conflict can interfere with quality decision making? | 140 |
| What attitudes are essential to effective conflict resolution? | 140 |
| What process activities can help promote conflict resolution? | 141 |

## CHAPTER NINE
# Group Processes for Goal Setting and Planning: 153

| | |
|---|---:|
| What does a good goal look like? | 153 |
| What is the essence of planning? | 154 |
| What process activities can help you set appropriate goals and plan effectively? | 154 |

BIBLIOGRAPHY .................................................. 173
QUOTATION CITATIONS ..................................... 176
INDEX ................................................................ 178

# About the Author

**Elaine K. McEwan** is a private educational consultant with the McEwan-Adkins Group offering training for school districts in leadership and team building, writing workshops for children, and parenting seminars. A former teacher, librarian, principal, and assistant superintendent for instruction in a suburban Chicago school district, she is the author of nearly two dozen books including titles for parents and teachers (*Attention Deficit Disorder,* Harold Shaw) fiction for middle-grade students (*Joshua McIntire Series,* David C. Cook), and guides for administrators (*Seven Steps to Effective Instructional Leadership,* Scholastic). She is the education columnist for the *Oro Valley Explorer* (AZ) newspaper, a contributing editor to several parenting magazines on educational issues, and can be heard on a variety of syndicated radio programs helping parents solve schooling problems.

She was honored by the Illinois Principals Association as an outstanding instructional leader, by the Illinois State Board of Education with an Award of Excellence in the Those Who Excel Program, and by the National Association of Elementary School Principals as the National Distinguished Principal from Illinois for 1991.

She received her undergraduate degree in education from Wheaton College and graduate degrees in library science and educational administration from Northern Illinois University.

McEwan lives with her husband and business partner E. Raymond Adkins in Oro Valley, Arizona.

# INTRODUCTION

As a brand-new principal in the fall of 1983, I was armed with a newly acquired doctorate in educational administration and all of the answers. My training program had included some passing references to participatory management and group decision making, but my job description led me to believe that I alone was responsible for what transpired in my school building. To compound my misguided approach to leadership, I was advised by the superintendent that my building had several ineffective teachers who needed a firm hand. I marched in to do battle without realizing that the troops were not behind me. Fortunately, I was rescued from imminent disaster when the concept of Building Leadership Teams was introduced to our district. After a brief training period, this team of four teachers and I spent one afternoon per month charting a course for school improvement and tackling the substantive issues of teaching and learning. We took our plans and recommendations to the faculty and learned many painful lessons about consensus building and conflict resolution. As a Building Leadership Team and faculty, we learned about the power of group decision making and as a principal, I learned how truly exhilarating leading a team to excellence can be. I learned how to empower teachers, how to listen to them, how to problem solve and plan with them, and how to envision with them the possibilities for the future. I also learned that sharing the responsibility with a leadership team, and in turn the entire faculty, improves the quality and authenticity of every decision. When I became an Assistant Superintendent for Instruction, I took my beliefs with me and implemented them with citizens' groups, the administrative council, faculty advisory groups, and curriculum committees. In my early days in administration, I would often break out in a cold sweat when faced with a particularly perplexing problem. Now I rest secure in the knowledge that the "team," whether it be a group of pupil personnel support staff conducting a particularly difficult staffing, a curriculum committee deadlocked over the choice of a program, a community group writing interdisciplinary outcomes, a faculty advisory council making recommendations on the staff development calendar, or a team of teachers revising the report card, will solve the problem. They will make a quality recommendation that all can support. They will rise to excellence.

Current educational journals are filled with articles about site-based management, school improvement teams, local school councils, teacher empowerment, and parent involvement. This is a concept whose time has surely come. But where will principals, teachers, central office administrators, community members, school board members, and parents find the help they need to skillfully lead their teams to excellence?

The chapters that follow contain a wide variety of group processes, organized to help you choose those that will best meet your needs. I have identified eight different types of team activities in which groups may engage over the course of their working life. Each of the following chapters contains one of the process types and can be read independently. Since there is always some sense of chronology in the "lifetime" of a working team, you may benefit from reading all of the chapters from start to finish, but you will not need to in order to use *Leading Your Team to Excellence* effectively.

I have written *Leading Your Team to Excellence: How to Make Quality Decisions* with five goals. These are to 1) convince you of the passion, power, and productivity that you can unleash in yourself and others through participatory decision making; 2) introduce and explore the concept of teaming; 3) describe and elaborate the decision-making process; 4) equip you with a repertoire of skills and processes to use with a variety of decision-making teams; and 5) to enable you to choose the appropriate skill and process for every decision-making situation.

Chapter One introduces you to the concept of teaming and discusses the decision-making process in depth. Chapters Two through Nine describe eight different types of team activities in which groups may engage over the course of their "working life" together. Chapter Two discusses building and sharing values, an important first step for any team that will be working together over a long period. Chapter Three covers team building and offers a variety of activities that, while not specifically focused on decision making, are designed to help a team build trust and teamwork. Chapter Four treats the important area of creativity and the generation of new ideas. When different approaches to problem solving are needed, the activities in this chapter will help your team rise to the occasion. Chapter Five describes ways in which groups can share critical information with one another and with the larger audiences they may be representing. In Chapter Six you will be introduced to problem-solving processes—ways in which your team can organize to tackle problems. Chapter Seven treats the important issue of consensus building and describes multiple ways in which to reach accord. When conflict arises, and it inevitably will, Chapter Eight will provide specific ways in which your team can resolve conflicts and facilitate conflict resolution in larger groups. Chapter Nine describes a variety of ways to engage in goal setting and planning.

Before you begin reading, please note the following caveats:

- Please read this book creatively with pen or highlighter in hand. The suggestions and activities are meant to be used to meet the needs of you and your group. They are not prescriptive, merely suggestive. Use what works; change what doesn't. Adopt, modify, and above all, create. All of the process activities contained in the book were developed by individuals working with groups who recognized a need for specific tools to help these groups be more effective. You will no doubt create your own tools as you become proficient in working with your team.

- I will refer to the group leader throughout the book. The leader could be a principal leading a School Leadership Team, a superintendent leading an administrative council, a director of instruction working with a curriculum committee, a parent leading a local school council, or a teacher working with a subject matter department or grade level team. The formal role of group leader should fall to almost everyone in the organization at one time or another. That's the wonder of shared leadership. However, if the examples don't always seem to fit your leadership role, just make up your own in your head as you read.

- I will also refer to teams throughout the book. These teams might be local school councils, school leadership teams, high school subject matter departments, elementary grade-level teams, single-issue task forces, curriculum development or selection committees, administrative councils or cabinets, boards of education, assessment and referral teams, teacher assistance teams, ad hoc problem-solving teams, middle school teaching teams, parent advisory groups, community advisory groups, quality circles, site-based management teams, child-study teams, school improvement teams, or boards of educational foundations.

- This book does not come with a money-back guarantee. Just as reading a diet book without commitment and sacrifice will not result in weight loss, reading this book without commitment and sacrifice won't result in quality decisions. Be prepared to make mistakes and encounter roadblocks along the way while leading your team to excellence. But also be prepared for good times, shared success, and the thrill of a job well done—together.

- Don't bother to read this book if you don't have at least a kernel of passion for the power of group decision making. If in your heart of hearts you still believe that this "committee stuff" is all a waste of time, then save your energy and close the covers of *Leading Your Team to Excellence* now.
- Just because an activity or process has worked well with one group, don't expect the same degree of success every time. Although there are some definite common traits among teams, every group responds differently to a specific process. Be flexible, be prepared to admit you've made a mistake, and be humble.
- Please don't read this book from cover to cover, beginning to end. It is not a novel, but rather a resource book. Once you've read Chapter One, flip through the rest of the book until you see something that interests you. Think of the current teams you are leading and the problems they may be having. Perhaps you can find a process or activity that will meet your immediate needs. Are you forming a new team in the near future? Consult the chapters that will assist you with getting your team off to the best possible start.
- Approach each new process with a sense of adventure and expectancy. Learn together with your team. There are two cases in which you should never use a brand-new (to you) process. These are when: 1) the team is newly formed and its members do not know each other well; or 2) the team is one with which you have never worked. In these cases stick with the tried-and-true approaches. New teams bring enough of their own surprises with them.
- Begin to look forward to team meetings with anticipation and excitement rather than dread. With the resources of *Leading Your Team to Excellence: How to Make Quality Decisions* at your fingertips, you will never be far from quality decision making.

To Raymond, who always makes quality decisions.

**CHAPTER ONE**

# Understanding Decision Making

**HOW DO DECISIONS ACTUALLY GET MADE?**

**WHAT IS QUALITY DECISION MAKING?**

**WHAT ARE THE ADVANTAGES OF TEAM DECISION MAKING?**

**WHAT CAN GO WRONG WITH DECISION MAKING?**

**WHEN SHOULD DECISIONS BE MADE BY A TEAM?**

**WHAT KINDS OF DECISIONS SHOULD BE MADE BY A TEAM?**

**WHAT DOES A GOOD TEAM LOOK LIKE?**

**HOW CAN YOU CONDUCT AN EFFECTIVE MEETING?**

**WHAT IS A GROUP PROCESS?**

**HOW CAN YOU SELECT A GROUP PROCESS TO MEET YOUR NEEDS?**

**ARE YOU READY TO BEGIN?**

## How do decisions actually get made?

Take a moment to think about where you work—your school, your office, your district. Have you ever stopped to consider how the important decisions really get made? When the organization moves forward, where has the impetus come from? From an individual or a group? Do things just happen, leaving you to wonder, "Now where did that come from?" Or does change occur through an orderly and systematic process that allows time and space for collaboration and consensus? Johnson and Johnson have identified seven different decision-making methods, and I have included three others from an additional source. As they are described, reflect on how decisions are made in your work, your family, and the community groups to which you belong. Think about the advantages and disadvantages of each of the following methods and the personal reaction you would have to an important decision made by one of these methods, especially if you were asked to fully support and implement that decision.

- **Decision by Authority Without Group Discussion** is an efficient method that gets the job done fast. However, for all but the most simple and routine decisions, this practice can leave group members wondering what is happening and why.[1]

> All decisions should be made as low as possible in the organization. The Charge of the Light Brigade was ordered by an officer who wasn't there looking at the territory.
> ——Robert Townsend

- **Decision by Default** occurs when a decision is arrived at by not making a decision. This may seem contradictory, but not making a decision is, in fact, choosing a course of action—to do nothing. Doing nothing may be an appropriate response to a situation, but decisions arrived at by default can also leave people confused.

- **Self-Authorized Decisions** are those made by one or more members of a group who assume that they have the authority to do so, but who actually do not. Such decisions can even come as a surprise to other group members, and chances are these other members will have little commitment to decisions made in this fashion.

- **Decisions by a Clique** are those decisions made by a few individuals who have joined forces and who then try to impose their view on others. These kinds of decisions can result in dividing the group into competing factions.[2]

- **Decision by Expert** is a method that begs the question of who is the expert. Is it the person with the knowledge and experience, the person with the power, or the person with the title?

- **Decision by Averaging Individuals' Opinions** is done by separately asking each group member for his or her opinion and then averaging the results. Although group members are consulted in this method, the opinions of both extremes tend to cancel out one another, and group members have no involvement in making the actual decision. Asking an expert to make the decision is almost preferable since at least a person with knowledge and information will be making the decision.

- **Decision by Authority After Group Discussion** allows for open discussion and information sharing by the group. This process can inform the authority and shape his or her opinion, but the ultimate decision rests with this individual. A danger in this method is that the discussion can evolve into either a competition for the ear of the authority or, even worse, telling the authority what the group thinks he or she wants to hear.

- **Decision by Minority** can occur when a subcommittee or executive committee makes most or all of the decisions for a group. While decision by minority is certainly a legitimate decision-making method, it can often take

> It's easy to get the players. Getting 'em to play together; that's the hard part.
> —Casey Stengel

place in illegitimate ways as well, such as the railroading that can often occur when two group members have come to agreement either prior to or during the meeting. This type of decision method may leave other group members scratching their heads after a meeting and wondering just what happened.

- **Decision by Majority Vote** is the most commonly used method in the United States. Majority voting has some major disadvantages when decision quality and buy-in are needed. If everyone's commitment is not important, however, this method works efficiently.

- **Decision by Consensus** is the method that will result in the highest quality decisions, but it will also take the most time. Consensus is usually defined as "a collective opinion arrived at by a group of individuals working together under conditions that permit communications to be sufficiently open—and the group climate to be sufficiently supportive—for everyone in the group to feel that he has had his fair chance to influence the decision."[3] (A more in-depth discussion of consensus will follow in Chapter Seven.) The ability to bring a group to consensus is one of the most important leadership skills needed by today's educational leaders. Consensus decision making is the best method for leading groups to the creative and quality decisions called for in the complex arena of educational reform.[4]

Consensus decision making, shared decision making, participatory management, and collaborative teaming are all synonymous with a process in which a variety of members of a given community (either a district, a school, a grade level, a subject matter department, a cross-disciplinary team, a student support team, or the community at large) collaborate, where appropriate, in identifying problems, defining goals, reaching consensus on policy, planning, and ensuring decision implementation. The community members become stakeholders in the decision.

## What is quality decision making?

Decisions are like gears moving our lives along, or, in some cases, jamming up and grinding us to a screeching halt. Whether to take a new job, move to another state, wear the navy or the gray suit, get married or stay single, or even to procrastinate on making any decision—decisions pile up as relentlessly as dirty laundry. Alarmed, we survey the mess and try to clean it up, sometimes with disastrous results. We can all point to the classic bad decisions—the Bay of Pigs disaster, President Carter's Iranian rescue mission, Ford's Edsel, and Coke's switch to New Coke™. Good decision making, however, is taken for granted.

Decision making, whether snap or deliberated, has long fascinated researchers—hence the reams of scholarly books and papers that line the library shelves in fields like psychology, economics, statistics, philosophy, and education. Making quality decisions is like picking winning stocks: If it were easy, everyone would be rich. However, understanding the stages of decision making will give you a good start.

> Decision making is a process by which a person, group, or organization identifies a choice or judgment to be made, gathers and evaluates information about alternatives, and selects from among the alternatives.
> —John S. Carroll and Eric J. Johnson

A quality decision, contrary to what you might first think, is not one in which the outcomes are all positive. Rather, a quality decision is one in which the decision makers have carried out all of the essential steps of the process. Decisions should not merely be judged on the basis of their outcome (either favorable or unfavorable), but on the basis of the process used in making the decision.[5] When decision makers ignore factual information or hurry through the process and fail to consider all of the options available, that's a bad decision. A sound decision that results in an undesirable outcome cannot necessarily be characterized as a poor decision because every decision involves a measure of risk. No one can foretell the future.

Researchers differ on the number of stages in the decision-making process and on precisely what takes place in each stage, but there is general agreement on the following basic stages:

- Figuring out that a decision is needed
- Generating/exploring/researching the alternative solutions/choices that might be made
- Making a judgment (yes or no regarding a single alternative) or a choice (comparing many alternatives)
- Acting upon the decision
- Evaluating the decision

## What are the advantages of team decision making?

The reasons for using team decision making are myriad and sound. Of course, there is the key reason that was stated earlier: People will be more committed to implementation if they are involved from the beginning in making the decision. And shared decision making has also been shown to build support, competence, and commitment,[6] increase job satisfaction,[7] create ownership leading to a more positive attitude toward the organization,[8] and create a more professional environment within the school.[9]

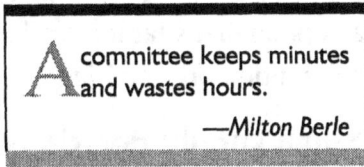

A committee keeps minutes and wastes hours.
—Milton Berle

Thomas Gordon in his book *Leader Effectiveness Training* adds these additional reasons for teaming:

- When group members participate in solving the group's problems, they learn a great deal about the technical complexities of whatever the group's task is; they learn from each other, as well as from the leader. *Developing a management team is the best kind of ongoing staff development.*

- Participation on a management team provides opportunities for members to *satisfy many of their higher-level needs* for self-esteem, acceptance, and self-actualization.

- A management team becomes the principal vehicle by which the leader exemplifies the kind of leadership he or she wants the group members to learn and use in relationships with *their* subordinates. In this way effective leadership moves down through the levels of organization.[10]

Shared decision making is also seen as a necessary precursor to school restructuring and educational reform. There are many who believe that shared decision making is a moral imperative, critical for the survival of the United States as a world leader.

To summarize, there are three big reasons (for you as leader) to use shared decision making with your team: 1) quality of decisions; 2) organizational effectiveness; and 3) staff satisfaction.

## What can go wrong with decision making?

There are really only two things that can go wrong with your team's decision making: either a decision doesn't get made at all or a bad decision is made. Either way, you have a problem. Some of us have avoided decisions by falling into the traps of complacency (like ignoring the need to examine the impact of gangs because we know it can't happen in our school), procrastination (putting off tackling the departmental reorganization that needs to happen because we just don't have the time right now), rationalization (if I make waves now, it will look bad on my evaluation), or passing the buck (blaming low student achievement on lack of parental involvement).

But many more of us are likely to have fallen into the "bad decision" traps like solving the wrong problem, failing to get all of the key players involved, going for an option that's far too obvious, overreacting to pressure and stress, relying strictly on intuition or "good judgment," and not learning from past mistakes.

## When should decisions be made by a team?

Shared decision making can sound like a panacea for every organizational ill, but imagine the organization where every decision is made by a team. Productivity would grind to a standstill and every available moment would be consumed with committee meetings. Perhaps you feel that your school or district has already arrived at this state of consensus chaos or group gridlock. But worse still, imagine the organization where all decisions are made by administrative fiat. Many of us have had traumatic experiences in working conditions like that and would not wish to relive them.

Team decision making will be most effective in organizations (districts, schools, communities) where shared decision making is modeled from the top down and strong school board/superintendent/teacher union/parent partnerships exist. Attempting widespread team decision making in one part of an organization, when the overall culture does not support or value this behavior, will be extremely difficult, although not impossible.

> Two can accomplish more than twice as much as one, for the results can be much better. If one falls, the other pulls him up; but if a man falls when he is alone, he's in trouble... And one standing alone can be attacked and defeated, but two can stand back-to-back and conquer; three is even better, for a triple-braided cord is not easily broken.
> —*Ecclesiastes 4:9–3*

## What kinds of decisions should be made by a team?

Many school improvement and leadership teams fall into the trap of applying their shared decision making skills (wonderful though they be) to tasks/problems/goals that have no educational relevance. Evaluate your choice of goals against these key questions:

### WILL THIS GOAL, IF ACCOMPLISHED, SOLVE AN IMPORTANT EDUCATIONAL PROBLEM?

Will it result in better teaching and learning? Beware of questions, issues, and problems that are mundane (the playground schedule isn't working; shall we participate in the DAR essay contest this year?); nonsensical (someone keeps parking in my spot and furthermore the lunch portions in the cafeteria are getting smaller); or distractive (kids just aren't as well behaved as they used to be, or, we did this back in the '60s and it didn't work then). Many long-standing teams become bogged down in "administrivia" (especially administrative teams) and lose sight of their original mission.

### DOES THIS GOAL WORK AT CROSS PURPOSES WITH THE WORK OF ANY OTHER GROUP?

Is the issue being studied by someone else? Redesigning a program when new state guidelines are about to be passed is an example of counterproductivity.

### CAN A PORTION OF THE GOAL BE ACCOMPLISHED WITHIN A REASONABLE PERIOD OF TIME?

Team members will need to see progress or other issues and projects will divert their energies.

### IS THIS GOAL ONE THAT WILL CONSUME THE PASSION, INTEREST, AND ATTENTION OF THE GROUP BECAUSE OF ITS RELEVANCE?

Make sure your goal isn't one that will evaporate into thin air when the meeting is over because no one really cares.

### IS THIS GOAL A DESIRED SOLUTION OR AN ATTEMPT TO FIND THE DESIRED SOLUTION?

An example of the former would be to design an after-school staff development program; an example of the latter would be to explore options to provide staff development for teachers.

## What does a good team look like?

Much has been written about the ideal team, but I have seldom had the opportunity of working with such a group. There have always been at least one or two individuals on every team or committee on which I've worked who made me fantasize about murder on a dark night. But our job as leaders is to lay aside the personalities and focus on the group behaviors that are essential to quality decisions. The following ideal characteristics that every team should possess may take some time to nurture and develop:

> Lou makes all the big decisions . . . like should we have a trade agreement with China, should we set up a space station on the moon. He leaves all the little decisions to me . . . like where we should live, where we should send the kids to school.
> 
> —*Virginia Simon*

- **Trust**—people can state their views and differences openly without fear of ridicule or retaliation and let others do the same.
- **Support**—people can get help from others on the team and give help without being concerned about hidden agendas.
- **Communication**—because of mutual trust, people can say what they feel.

- **Team objectives**—with each team objective, people work through their differences until they can honestly say they are committed to achieving the objective.
- **Conflict resolution skills**—people do not suppress conflicts or pretend they do not exist. Instead, they work through them openly.
- **Utilization of members**—the individual abilities, knowledge, and experience of the team members are fully utilized.
- **Control**—everyone accepts the responsibility for keeping communication relevant and the team operation on track.
- **Climate**—the team "climate" is one of openness and respectfulness of individual differences.

Management theorist Douglas McGregor's description of an effective work group remains a classic contribution to the research on group behavior. It is presented here in an abbreviated form.[11]

1. The atmosphere tends to be informal, comfortable, and relaxed.
2. There is a lot of discussion in which virtually everyone participates.
3. The task or objective of the group is well understood and accepted.
4. The members listen to each other.
5. There is disagreement.
6. Most decisions are reached by a kind of consensus.
7. Criticism is frequent, frank, and participants are comfortable with it.
8. People are free in expressing their feelings as well as their ideas.
9. When action is taken, clear assignments are made and accepted.
10. The chair does not dominate, nor does the group defer to him or her.
11. The group frequently examines how well it is doing and what may be interfering with its operation.[12]

One need only consider the reverse of these characteristics to paint a thumbnail sketch of the ineffective group. We've all been a part of such a group at least once in our careers and can still remember the pain of attending meetings under conditions best compared to having a root canal or hearing a child's fingernails scratch down the chalkboard. You can re-create all too readily the domination by the leader, the warring cliques and subgroups, the unequal participation and uneven use of group resources, the rigid or dysfunctional group norms and procedures, the climate of defensiveness or fear, the uncreative alternatives to problems, the restricted communications, and the avoidance of differences or potential conflicts.[13] Just writing about them is enough to give me sweaty palms and a headache.

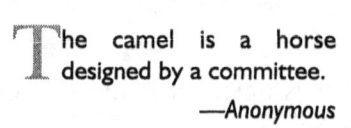

The camel is a horse designed by a committee.
—Anonymous

## How can you conduct an effective meeting?

Volumes have been written about effective meetings, but one of the best is *How to Make Meetings Work* (1986) by Michael Doyle and David Straus. Their eighteen steps to a better meeting have been my "bible" as a meeting facilitator.[14] I won't say that I always manage to hit every point, but when I don't, the members of my group and I always pay the price. I do, without fail, start my meetings on time. I don't care if only one person is there, we begin. Because if I don't, the next time that person will be late and thus begins an endless cycle of late-comers to meetings. (I sometimes fudge on cleaning up and rearranging the room. I don't want to be accused of taking work away from the building maintenance crew.) Here are the eighteen steps:

**BEFORE THE MEETING**
1. Plan the meeting carefully: who, what, when, where, why, how many.
2. Prepare and send out an agenda in advance.
3. Come early and set up the meeting room.

**AT THE BEGINNING OF THE MEETING**
4. Start on time.
5. Get participants to introduce themselves and state their expectations for the meeting. (Applicable only for a newly formed group unless there are new members.)
6. Clearly define roles.
7. Review, revise, and order the agenda.
8. Set clear time limits.
9. Review action items from the previous meeting.

**DURING THE MEETING**
10. Focus on the same problem in the same way at the same time.

**AT THE END OF THE MEETING**
11. Establish action items: who, what, when.
12. Review the group memory.
13. Set the date and place of the next meeting and develop a preliminary agenda.
14. Evaluate the meeting.
15. Close the meeting crisply and positively.
16. Clean up and rearrange the room.

**AFTER THE MEETING**
17. Prepare the group memo.
18. Follow up on action items and begin to plan the next meeting.

I believe one of the most crucial points that Doyle and Straus make in their book deals with the concept of "group memory." You must read their Chapter Seven yourself to appreciate the importance of "group memory," but I will try to summarize the high points for you. The group memory is captured by a recorder, an individual who takes "big notes" on chart paper, newsprint, or butcher paper. This individual keeps a running record of the group's proceedings, which serves as a powerful visual tool to help members concentrate and see what is going on, as well as a ready-made instant replay of the entire meeting. No longer will you need to rely on your own short-term memory—you will have a large and very graphic display from which to work. The recorder of group memory is different from the old-fashioned group secretary (who was almost always a "her") who wrote her notes privately and then transcribed them with little or no accountability to the group for what she had written. Unless, of course, someone bothered to read them before the next meeting and offered a correction. The chart-paper record will be under constant scrutiny by the group and additions and corrections will be made as the meeting progresses. Many small teams have mounted mylar boards in their conference rooms, and while these are convenient, they do get erased and cannot be saved for future reference like the rolls of chart paper currently stacked in my office. Doyle and Straus say that almost anyone can learn to be an adequate recorder. In this case, the operable word is adequate. I've worked with some of the best. Their graphics, color-coordinated headings, and ability to capture the essence of a rambling statement are legendary. They underline, highlight, and use stars, arrows, and numbers. They twirl their markers like circus performers and are never embarrassed when they misspell a word. One district in which I worked even offered a "graphics workshop" specifically designed to enhance recording skills. It was a coveted opportunity and resulted in some outstanding recording of our administrative team meetings and leadership team planning meetings.

> It is logical that if you properly combine the judgment of a large number of people, you have a better chance of getting closer to the truth.
> —O. Helmer

## What is a group process?

One of the most important aspects of quality decision making is the effective use of "process." A process is an activity or structure that can help facilitate group decision making. The process can often be as important for the group as the product or outcome of their endeavor. Group leaders, rather than being experts with all of the answers, must become process experts. There are four things you will do as a process expert:

- Help your group to ask the right questions;
- Help your group to discuss and debate ideas openly and freely;

- Help to create a climate in which your group can make judgments and choices; and
- Help your group to commit to the implementation of their choices.

## How can you select a group process to meet your needs?

Selecting and effectively using the group process that will satisfy the demands of the task, the characteristics of your group, and your leadership abilities will be a challenge in the beginning if you have not done it before. Leading any group (even a familiar and very accepting group) through a new and untried process is like riding a bicycle or driving a "four on the floor" automobile in

> A committee is a group of people who individually do nothing but as a group decide that nothing can be done.
> —Fred Allen

the beginning stages of learning. There are many steps to the process, and while negotiating each of the steps you must watch out for the traffic, pedestrians, bumps in the road, and detours. Once the process has been learned and practiced, however, you will become skilled at using it with a variety of groups and in many settings. You will begin to experiment, revise, and develop processes of your own.

## Are you ready to begin?

A word of caution is in order before you begin. Why do some teams soar and others crash on the rocks? There are some pitfalls with shared decision making, and if you know what they are ahead of time, you, the group leader, can lead your team to excellence, rather than extinction. Just "doing" shared decision making isn't enough. You have to do it right!

There are four big roadblocks that can stand between you and quality decisions.

- **The lack of communication roadblock:** Keep group members sharing their ideas and exchanging information. If group members do not believe they have been listened to, they will soon become cynical, undermining, and, in some cases, downright dangerous. I have observed many site-based teams who were constituted by district directive and whose leaders were unwilling participants. The damage done by such a travesty will take another group leader years to repair.
- **The consensus at any costs roadblock:** Squelching disagreements through quick compromises or encouraging self-censorship by creating a climate that discourages conflict can be disastrous.
- **Organizational dissonance roadblock:** We've all known individuals who didn't "walk their talk," and it can happen in the arena of shared decision making—superintendents who say they believe participatory management is

desirable and effective, but who have low opinions of the abilities of teachers to make quality decisions, or principals who make all the decisions for their leadership groups in advance of the group meeting. If you know the answer to the question or the solution to the problem before your team meeting, then you might examine why you are even meeting. Your behavior will send a clear message that you have already made the decision and the group is merely there to determine how to implement it.

> Decisions should be judged on the basis of the processes used in making them.
> —Daniel D. Wheeler and Irving L. Janis

- **Confusing participation and participatory management roadblock:** If group members begin to believe that participation and participatory management are synonymous, they will become bitter and angry when their input isn't always used. Take great care to communicate at what level *participation* may or may not become *participatory decision making*.

With these words of warning sounding in your ears, you are ready to begin. Find a partner and work together. Share ideas, successes, and failures. Enlist your entire administrative team and focus on group facilitation and process consultation as an area of staff development for everyone.

---

[1] D. W. Johnson and F. P. Johnson, *Joining Together,* (Englewood Cliffs, New Jersey: Prentice Hall, Inc., 1982), 103–109.

[2] B. J. Hansen and C. L. Marburger, *School-Based Improvement,* (Columbia, Maryland: National Committee for Citizens in Education, 1989), 75.

[3] Johnson, op cit., 106.

[4] Ibid.

[5] D. D. Wheeler and I. L. Janis, *A Practical Guide for Making Decisions,* (New York: The Free Press, 1980), 5.

[6] Betty Dillon-Peterson, "Trusting Teachers To Know What's Good for Them." *Improving Teaching,* edited by Karen K. Zumwalt.( Alexandria, Virginia: ASCD, 1986), 29–35.

[7] P. T. Ashton and R. B. Webb, *Making a Difference,* (New York: Longman, 1986), 95–97.

[8] D. E. Beers, "School-Based Management." Paper presented at National Convention of the National Association of Elementary School Principals, New Orleans, 1984.

[9] Maja Apelman, "Working with Teachers: The Advisory Approach." *Improving Teaching,* edited by K. Zumwalt. (Alexandria, Virginia: ASCD, 1986), 115–129.

[10] T. Gordon, *Leader Effectiveness Training,* (New York: G. P. Putnam's Sons, 1977), 41.

[11] R. F. Lynch and T. J. Werner, *Continuous Improvement,* (Atlanta, Georgia: QualTeam Inc., 1992), 119–120.

[12] D. McGregor, *Human Side of Enterprise,* (New York: McGraw-Hill, 1960), 232–235.

[13] W. G. Dyer, *Team Building,* (Reading, Massachusetts: Addison-Wesley Publishing Company, 1977), 57.

[14] M. Doyle and D. Straus, *How to Make Meetings Work,* (New York: The Berkley Publishing Company, 1986), 289–290.

■ CHAPTER TWO

# Group Processes for Building and Sharing Values

---

**WHAT IS THE IMPORTANCE OF VALUES IN BUILDING A TEAM THAT IS CAPABLE OF QUALITY DECISIONS?**

**WHAT PROCESS ACTIVITIES CAN HELP MY TEAM TO BUILD AND SHARE VALUES?**

---

In a district where I once worked, a management consultant was hired to help remediate some problems that had arisen over the years. He spent a couple of hours with each member of the administrative team asking questions and listening. Then he planned a day-long retreat. Most people had been to administrative retreats before, but the reality of this day turned out to be very different from most and quite unsettling for some of the participants.

First we completed a values clarification instrument in which we were asked to carefully read ten items that each contained two statements representing polar-opposite positions on a value continuum. Upon completing the instrument we each developed a personal profile that showed where we were on a high-risk, low-risk continuum. In discussing our profiles we were able to see our similarities and differences as a team, and more importantly, the superintendent was able to communicate some important values regarding the organization and its future. We then looked at six areas of our lives: education, family, financial and career, health and fitness, social and cultural, and spiritual, and ranked each in terms of its importance in our "desired value system." We then did a second ranking of each item in terms of its importance in our "present value system." A final task included writing objectives under each area that would help us realize goals in the areas that were widely discrepant between desired and actual. There was some grumbling at the break time about this departure from our usual staff development activities. "I can't stand this 'touchy-feely' stuff," said one administrator. "What does this have to do with my job? We should do something that will help us be better principals," added another. Still another was silent, distressed at the unwelcome intervention by the consultant into how she managed her time, life, and relationships.

That particular session represented a turning point in our district. Some individuals realized their values were not congruent with the vision and mission of the organization and over time found other jobs. Those of us who remained talked about this experience many times. I personally still use the goal setting process in the six areas as a yearly "dipstick" of my personal growth.

> Giving shape and direction to a school's culture should be a clear, articulated vision of what the school stands for, a vision that embodies core values and purposes. Examples of core values might be community building, problem-solving skills, or effective communication. These value commitments vary from community to community; what is important for school leaders to know is the role of values as the fuel of school improvement. If core values are the fuel, then school culture is the engine.
>
> —Jon Saphier
> and Matthew King

## What is the importance of values in building a team that is capable of quality decisions?

The experience made me realize how important congruity of values can be in any kind of team. A value is a standard that we use to guide behavior. Values are not attitudes, opinions, or behavior traits. These three descriptors are merely value indicators. Because of our attitudes, opinions, and behavior traits, our friends and family can point to our underlying values.

Values development begins in early infancy and is shaped by all of the relationships we have—family, peers, teachers, friends, colleagues, institutions, and society at large. There are three accepted phases of value development: acceptance (the individual is willing to identify with the value, but can quickly reassess its worth if more desirable options present themselves); preference (the individual is committed enough to the value to pursue it); and commitment (the individual has such a degree of certainty about it that he or she will always act upon it with firm conviction and certainty).

Values are important in the decision-making process because they are the motivating factors in deciding which goals we will pursue and they serve as reference points for our own self-evaluation and definition. Values are also the standards by which we judge the decisions of others. Until I participated in the day-long workshop together with my fellow administrators, I had never had an opportunity to clarify my values for them, and the same was true of them for me. Discussing, sharing, and building values together is the first step in quality decision making.

## What process activities can help my team to build and share values?

The process activities that follow are designed to help your team share and build values. Some are very simple and can be completed in a short time. They will assist your team in sharing values and beliefs through brief exchanges and encounters. Others are designed to take several hours and may have the kind of life-changing impact that the process I described earlier had on me.

> Vision defines how our work contributes to the kind of life we want to live and that we want others to have . . . Its structure is less important than its effect on the values and behaviors of every member of the organization.
>
> —Robert F. Lynch and Thomas J. Werner

Each process will contain six easy-to-follow steps: 1. Description, 2. Application, 3. Time Required, 4. Group Size, 5. Materials, and 6. Process.

---

**PROCESS NUMBER 1    BUILDING AND SHARING VALUES**

## IF MY SCHOOL WERE . . .

### ■ DESCRIPTION

Individuals are asked to imagine that their school (or district, or community) is one of the following: a movie, a book, a car, a song, a sports team, a food, or a soap opera. In the course of this icebreaker, participants will share the title or name of the book, movie, etc. with the group and then briefly explain why they chose it.

### ■ APPLICATION

This process can be used when individuals from a variety of schools, districts, or communities come together for problem solving or goal development. It will enable them to share important information about their workplace in a timely and often humorous way. The process can also be used with a well-established group as a meeting ice-breaker.

### ■ TIME REQUIRED

Writing and debriefing this activity can take anywhere from ten to thirty minutes, depending on how many individuals share their ideas and how much discussion is generated.

### ■ GROUP SIZE

Five to thirty-five can participate in this activity. Use the "turn to your partner and share" technique for larger groups.

### ■ MATERIALS

Overhead, mylar board, chalkboard, or chart paper, and markers. A prepared handout can be used as well.

### ■ PROCESS

1. Ask group participants to put on their creative hats and imagine that their school (or district, or community) is a movie, a television sitcom, a book, a car, a song, a sports team, a food, or a soap opera. Give them some examples.

2. Some examples of responses might be: If my school were a movie, it would be *Stand and Deliver*; if my school were a soap opera, it would be *The Young and the Restless*; it were a car, it would be a Mustang.

3. Give participants a prepared sheet or ask them to write this statement down in their notes.

    If my school were a (movie, TV sitcom, book, etc.) it would be _____.

    Then ask them to fill in the blank with the title or name of an actual movie, TV sitcom, or book, etc.

4. As time permits, ask participants to explain the reasons behind their choices to the group. In large groups, ask people to share their responses with a partner. If teams of individuals from one school are sitting together, ask them to share and compare their answers.

<sub>Adapted from processes developed by Dr. Mary Weck, Assistant Superintendent for Human Resources, Downers Grove (IL) High School District, and Dr. Linda Murphy, Superintendent, Kenilworth Elementary District, Kenilworth (IL).</sub>

---

PROCESS NUMBER  BUILDING AND SHARING VALUES

# WHAT'S IN YOUR WALLET?

### ■ DESCRIPTION

What's in Your Wallet? is an icebreaker that asks each member of the group to remove something from his or her wallet that has significance and to describe what it is and its meaning to the group.

### ■ APPLICATION

This process can be used with a well-established group or one in which the participants have never met. Even in well-established groups, this exercise will often reveal material containing information that participants do not know about one another (e.g., mad money for use at the race track, a membership card of an organization, a family picture, etc.).

### ■ TIME REQUIRED
Ten to fifteen minutes.

### ■ GROUP SIZE
Ten to twenty people.

### ■ MATERIALS
None.

### ■ PROCESS
Ask participants to look through their wallets, remove something they value, and share the item's significance with the group.

---

**PROCESS NUMBER**  **BUILDING AND SHARING VALUES**

# TWO TRUTHS AND A LIE

### ■ DESCRIPTION
In Two Truths and a Lie individuals share two statements about themselves that are true and one that is not. Other members of the group try to determine which of the statements is not true.

### ■ APPLICATION
This process can be used with a well-established group or one in which the participants have never met before. Even in well-established groups, this exercise will often reveal information that participants do not know about one another (e.g., John was a cheerleader in high school, Mary played the drums in a rock band, or Phyllis lived next door to John Belushi when she was growing up).

### ■ TIME REQUIRED
Ten to twenty minutes.

### ■ GROUP SIZE
Ten to twenty people.

### ■ MATERIALS
None.

### ■ PROCESS
1. Ask each group member to write down three statements about himself or herself. Two of the statements should be true and one should be false.
2. When all participants have completed their statements, ask for volunteers to read their statements, and have the group members decide which one is the lie. The object of this "game" is to fool the participants with an outrageous truth and a very sensible and commonplace lie.

3. In larger groups, participants can share their two truths and a lie in small groups of three to five people.

## PROCESS NUMBER 4: BUILDING AND SHARING VALUES

### "WANTED...FOR"

### ■ DESCRIPTION
This process is a brief warm-up activity to encourage people to think about their own personal values. Participants are asked to make several brief statements about themselves that touch on values and beliefs.

### ■ APPLICATION
When individuals from a variety of schools, districts, or communities come together for problem solving, goal development, or any type of staff development activity, this activity will enable individuals to share important information about their workplace in a timely and often humorous way. The activity can also be used with a well-established group as a meeting icebreaker.

### ■ TIME REQUIRED
Ten to thirty minutes.

### ■ GROUP SIZE
Five to thirty-five people. Use the "turn to your partner and share" technique for larger groups.

### ■ MATERIALS
Form on which to record responses for each participant. See the handout.

### ■ PROCESS
1. Pass out the handout to each participant.
2. Give the following instructions to the group:
   - Take a few minutes and fill in the blanks of this Wanted Poster. You are the person who is wanted and you are wanted for four things:
     - for always being . . .
     - having strong needs for . . .
     - greatly valuing . . .
     - living by the slogan . . .
3. When participants have completed their Wanted Posters, share with partners, teams, or large group, depending on the setting.

*Adapted from Administrator's Academy: School Culture, a training session developed by Dr. Linda Murphy and Dr. Len Sirotski, Educational Service Region 4, DuPage County, Illinois.*

## WANTED... FOR

My name is _____

And I am wanted for:

- Always being _____
- Having strong needs for _____
- Greatly valuing _____
- Living by the slogan _____

SOURCE: Adapted from Administrator's Academy: School Culture, a training session developed by Dr. Linda Murphy and Dr. Len Sirotski, Educational Service Region 4, DuPage County, Illinois.

PROCESS NUMBER  BUILDING AND SHARING VALUES

# NAME TAG MIXER

### ■ DESCRIPTION

Name Tag Mixer is a quick and easy icebreaker that utilizes name tags to share personal and value based information about participants.

### ■ APPLICATION

Use with larger groups whose members are not well acquainted or who are total strangers.

### ■ TIME REQUIRED

Fifteen to twenty minutes.

### ■ GROUP SIZE

Ten to thirty people.

### ■ MATERIALS

A 4 × 6 plain notecard for each participant. Magic markers for each table. Masking tape to affix name tags to participants' clothing. Overhead, chalkboard, mylar board, or chart paper containing a name tag as an example for participants.

### ■ PROCESS

1. Have a large sample of the name tag prominently displayed so that individuals can begin writing their tag as they enter the room. Have 4 × 6 cards and magic markers at each table. Participants can affix their name tags to their clothing with masking tape. If you wish, the following directions can be duplicated for participants as well.

2. In the upper-left corner of the 4 × 6 card, write the name of a celebrity you would most like to meet. In the upper middle, write your favorite TV show or movie. In the upper-right corner, write what career you would have chosen, if not the one you presently have. In the middle right, write the name of a person you particularly admire. In the middle left, write a summer vacation experience you especially enjoyed. In the bottom left, write a talent you have that few of your colleagues realize you possess. In the bottom middle, write the name of the place where you would most like to retire. In the bottom right, write the name of an animal that best describes your personality.
3. Write your first name in large bold letters in the center of the card.
4. When all participants have arrived and completed their name tags, ask the members of each group/table to share the information with each other.

**SAMPLE NAME TAG**

| John Grisham | The Big Chill | Lawyer |
|---|---|---|
| Trip to Europe | **Elaine** | Billy Graham |
| Sewing | Tucson, AZ | Roadrunner |

**PROCESS NUMBER 6  BUILDING AND SHARING VALUES**

# COLLEGIALITY ASSESSMENT

## DESCRIPTION

The Collegiality Inventory is a twenty-item questionnaire designed to assess the level of collegiality among a staff or work group. The questionnaire will be completed privately and anonymously, collated by one or more individuals, and the information discussed and analyzed by the group.

## APPLICATION

The process is best used by a group that recognizes the need for better working relationships, but is not certain exactly where problems lie or what steps need to be taken. The instrument might also be helpful to a new administrator who wishes to assess conditions in a new work setting.

## TIME REQUIRED

Each individual will complete the questionnaire privately, which may take from ten to thirty minutes, depending on the amount of time each question is considered. Discussing and processing the results of the questionnaire may take from thirty minutes to one and one-half hours, if, as part of the processing, items will be identified for problem solving or action plans will be made.

## GROUP SIZE

Any size. Once the results have been collated, however, a smaller leadership group may more efficiently deal with the issues and problems identified.

## MATERIALS

Copy of the Collegiality Inventory for each participant.

## PROCESS

1. While you could pass out the questionnaire through individual mailboxes, it will be preferable to pass it out in a brief meeting to explain the purpose of the questionnaire, who will collate the results, and how the results will be used.
2. Designate two or three individuals who will collect the questionnaires. Provide each of them with a large manila envelope, which they will place in their mailboxes. As group members complete the questionnaire, they will place it in one of the envelopes.
3. When all group members have completed the questionnaire, the individuals who collected them will collate the information for presentation to the large group.

**4.** Follow-up activities to the administration of this questionnaire are crucial. Asking for and then not using this kind of information will certainly not improve collegiality, and you risk losing your credibility. If you have no intention of using the information to bring about change in attitudes and behaviors with regard to collegiality, then won't want to hand out the questionnaire. The next time you really need information from people, they won't want to complete the questionnaire because you've lost your credibility.

Adapted from Administrator's Academy: School Culture, a training session developed by<br>Dr. Linda Murphy and Dr. Len Sirotski, Educational Service Region 4, DuPage County, Illinois.

## COLLEGIALITY INVENTORY

Place an × on one of the five dots on each line immediately after each statement indicating your sense of the frequency of the situation or behavior among your staff or work group.

1. There is a free flow of ideas.

   HARDLY EVER — NOT OFTEN — AS OFTEN AS NOT — QUITE OFTEN — ALMOST ALWAYS

2. Ideas are judged on their merit rather than their source.

   HARDLY EVER — NOT OFTEN — AS OFTEN AS NOT — QUITE OFTEN — ALMOST ALWAYS

3. Rules do not define what we do as much as our beliefs about what needs to be done together.

   HARDLY EVER — NOT OFTEN — AS OFTEN AS NOT — QUITE OFTEN — ALMOST ALWAYS

4. Our meetings include everyone who needs to attend.

   HARDLY EVER — NOT OFTEN — AS OFTEN AS NOT — QUITE OFTEN — ALMOST ALWAYS

5. Colleagues are not simply co-workers, but rather professional friends.

   HARDLY EVER — NOT OFTEN — AS OFTEN AS NOT — QUITE OFTEN — ALMOST ALWAYS

6. We respect teachers as the central professionals in the school district.

   HARDLY EVER — NOT OFTEN — AS OFTEN AS NOT — QUITE OFTEN — ALMOST ALWAYS

7. Authority and responsibility are shared.

   HARDLY EVER — NOT OFTEN — AS OFTEN AS NOT — QUITE OFTEN — ALMOST ALWAYS

8. Decisions are made by those most capable of making them.

   HARDLY EVER — NOT OFTEN — AS OFTEN AS NOT — QUITE OFTEN — ALMOST ALWAYS

## COLLEGIALITY INVENTORY–Cont.

9. This is a learning organization, one where personal and professional growth are encouraged.

   HARDLY EVER — NOT OFTEN — AS OFTEN AS NOT — QUITE OFTEN — ALMOST ALWAYS

10. We take adequate time to discuss issues, reflect on them, and plan together.

    HARDLY EVER — NOT OFTEN — AS OFTEN AS NOT — QUITE OFTEN — ALMOST ALWAYS

11. Our organization is flat, rather than layered in a pyramid style.

    HARDLY EVER — NOT OFTEN — AS OFTEN AS NOT — QUITE OFTEN — ALMOST ALWAYS

12. The role of the administrator as facilitator is encouraged.

    HARDLY EVER — NOT OFTEN — AS OFTEN AS NOT — QUITE OFTEN — ALMOST ALWAYS

13. The organization seems as committed to us as we are to it.

    HARDLY EVER — NOT OFTEN — AS OFTEN AS NOT — QUITE OFTEN — ALMOST ALWAYS

14. Cooperation is praised openly.

    HARDLY EVER — NOT OFTEN — AS OFTEN AS NOT — QUITE OFTEN — ALMOST ALWAYS

15. Administrators model collegiality for teachers.

    HARDLY EVER — NOT OFTEN — AS OFTEN AS NOT — QUITE OFTEN — ALMOST ALWAYS

16. Thoughtful listening is appreciated.

    HARDLY EVER — NOT OFTEN — AS OFTEN AS NOT — QUITE OFTEN — ALMOST ALWAYS

17. Volunteerism is a hallmark of the way we work together, and it is sincere.

    HARDLY EVER — NOT OFTEN — AS OFTEN AS NOT — QUITE OFTEN — ALMOST ALWAYS

18. We have a collective sense of ownership.

    HARDLY EVER — NOT OFTEN — AS OFTEN AS NOT — QUITE OFTEN — ALMOST ALWAYS

19. We take more risks together than we might individually.

    HARDLY EVER — NOT OFTEN — AS OFTEN AS NOT — QUITE OFTEN — ALMOST ALWAYS

20. Consensus, rather than compromise, guides our decision-making style.

    HARDLY EVER — NOT OFTEN — AS OFTEN AS NOT — QUITE OFTEN — ALMOST ALWAYS

SOURCE: Adapted from Administrator's Academy: School Culture, a training session developed by Dr. Linda Murphy and Dr. Len Sirotski, Educational Service Region 4, Du Page County, Illinois. Reprinted by permission.

**PROCESS NUMBER 7  BUILDING AND SHARING VALUES**

# SCHOOL CULTURE ASSESSMENT

### ■ DESCRIPTION

This activity is a questionnaire on which individuals assess the quality of their workplace based on twelve cultural norms that affect school improvement as identified by Jon Saphier and Matthew King. Following completion of the assessment, individuals choose three norms that they believe are the most important and identify conditions that weaken the cultural norm and conditions that strengthen it.

### ■ APPLICATION

This process would be used most effectively with a school faculty or school leadership team to determine where significant changes are needed in the culture.

### ■ TIME REQUIRED

Thirty to forty-five minutes.

### ■ GROUP SIZE

Any size group. Once the results have been collated, however, a smaller leadership group may more efficiently deal with the issues and problem identified.

### ■ MATERIALS

Copies of the Twelve Norms of School Culture, the inventory for each participant, and two copies of the worksheet for each participant. Reprints of the *Educational Leadership* article from which the norms are taken are optional. (See Bibliography.)

### ■ PROCESS

1. Distribute copies of the following list by Jon Saphier and Matthew King (The Twelve Norms of School Culture) and give a brief explanation of what each cultural norm means. If possible, give specific examples from your school site to illustrate each norm. If Saphier and King's work is not familiar to you, obtain a copy of the article to read.
2. Pass out copies of the Norms of School Culture Inventory.
3. Instructions to Group: Take forty-five minutes to work alone, silently recording your thoughts, feelings, and ideas on the sheets provided.
   - First, rate all twelve norms of school culture on a 1 to 5 scale by placing an × on the location that best describes the strength of that norm in your present school site. What you're doing is giving a quick reaction to how strong you think each norm is right now among the staff here at our school.

- Next, pick three of these norms that you think are the most important to the staff here at the school. *Most important* could mean those norms that are currently responsible for the school's strengths, or it could mean those norms that are most in need of attention.
- Complete one worksheet for each norm you choose. Pass out two copies of the worksheet to each participant.
- Write down the practices or conditions you can think of that currently strengthen this norm (the one you're writing about at the moment).
- These sheets are for guiding your thinking and will not be collected. It is important, however, to the success of the group discussions that will follow that you really use this forty-five minutes of alone-time productively and not break off into discussions too early. It is also important that you do some writing during this time to facilitate your thinking.

4. Move about the room to answer questions and monitor productivity.
5. When everyone has completed the questionnaires, take a few moments to poll the large group (one minute) to determine which norms were most frequently chosen. Then break into small groups of three to five individuals. Take care to divide the groups heterogenously (across grade levels, departments, specialties) so that each group will be representative. The purpose of the discussion will be to share information, ideas, and suggestions, not to develop any action plans.
6. Give the following instructions to the group:
   - Appoint a recorder and facilitator in each small group. Record the norms and the frequency with which they were chosen. Share ideas and suggestions in the small groups. Your job is not to solve problems or develop action plans. The information that is recorded will be collated and discussed by the school leadership team.
7. Thank the group members for their input and inform them of the timelines for discussing and dealing with the information they have shared.

## THE TWELVE NORMS OF SCHOOL CULTURE

- **Collegiality**—Teachers helping teachers; administrators helping teachers; teachers helping administrators.

- **Experimentation**—An openness to new ideas and the motivation to try them.

- **High Expectations**—Standards of excellence for administrators, teachers, and students.

- **Trust and Confidence**—Commitment to one another and a willingness to be open and vulnerable.

- **Tangible Support**—Resources to get the job done.

- **Reaching Out to the Knowledge Base**—Constant learning about new teaching and learning strategies.

- **Appreciation and Recognition**—People appreciate people, and the appreciation is public.

- **Caring, Celebration, and Humor**—People who work together have fun.

- **Involvement in Decision Making**—Shared consensus.

- **Protection of What's Important**—Teaching and learning are priorities.

- **Traditions**—Something special is always going on.

- **Honest and Open Communication**—Everyone's opinion counts.

SOURCE: Saphier, J., and M. King, "Good Seeds Grow in Strong Cultures." *Educational Leadership*, 42 (6), 67. Copyright © 1985 by ASCD. Reprinted by permission. All rights reserved.

## NORMS OF SCHOOL CULTURE INVENTORY

Directions: Rate the twelve norms of school culture by placing an × on the location that best describes the presence of that norm in your present school site.

1. **Collegiality: Teachers helping teachers; administrators helping teachers; teachers helping administrators.**

   HARDLY EVER — NOT OFTEN — AS OFTEN AS NOT — QUITE OFTEN — ALMOST ALWAYS

## NORMS OF SCHOOL CULTURE INVENTORY—Cont.

2. **Experimentation:** An openness to new ideas and the motivation to try them.

   HARDLY EVER — NOT OFTEN — AS OFTEN AS NOT — QUITE OFTEN — ALMOST ALWAYS

3. **High Expectations:** Standards of excellence for administrators, teachers, and students.

   HARDLY EVER — NOT OFTEN — AS OFTEN AS NOT — QUITE OFTEN — ALMOST ALWAYS

4. **Trust and Confidence:** Commitment to one another and a willingness to be open and vulnerable.

   HARDLY EVER — NOT OFTEN — AS OFTEN AS NOT — QUITE OFTEN — ALMOST ALWAYS

5. **Tangible Support:** Resources to get the job done.

   HARDLY EVER — NOT OFTEN — AS OFTEN AS NOT — QUITE OFTEN — ALMOST ALWAYS

6. **Reaching Out to the Knowledge Base:** Constant learning about new teaching and learning strategies.

   HARDLY EVER — NOT OFTEN — AS OFTEN AS NOT — QUITE OFTEN — ALMOST ALWAYS

7. **Appreciation and Recognition:** People appreciate people, and the appreciation is public.

   HARDLY EVER — NOT OFTEN — AS OFTEN AS NOT — QUITE OFTEN — ALMOST ALWAYS

8. **Caring, Celebration, and Humor:** People who work together have fun.

   HARDLY EVER — NOT OFTEN — AS OFTEN AS NOT — QUITE OFTEN — ALMOST ALWAYS

9. **Involvement in Decision Making:** Shared consensus.

   HARDLY EVER — NOT OFTEN — AS OFTEN AS NOT — QUITE OFTEN — ALMOST ALWAYS

10. **Protection of What's Important:** Teaching and learning are priorities.

    HARDLY EVER — NOT OFTEN — AS OFTEN AS NOT — QUITE OFTEN — ALMOST ALWAYS

11. **Traditions:** Something special is always going on.

    HARDLY EVER — NOT OFTEN — AS OFTEN AS NOT — QUITE OFTEN — ALMOST ALWAYS

12. **Honest and Open Communication:** Everyone's opinion counts.

    HARDLY EVER — NOT OFTEN — AS OFTEN AS NOT — QUITE OFTEN — ALMOST ALWAYS

SOURCE: Adapted from Saphier, J., and M. King, "Good Seeds Grow in Strong Cultures." *Educational Leadership,* 42 (6), 67. Copyright © 1985 by ASCD.

### NORMS OF SCHOOL CULTURE WORKSHEET

Norm:

What practices or conditions in my school currently strengthen this norm?

What practices or conditions in my school currently weaken this norm?

What is my vision of what this norm could be at its best?

What ideas do I have to improve this norm?

What would I be willing to do to improve this norm?

SOURCE: Developed by Dr. Linda Murphy. Reprinted by permission.

## PROCESS NUMBER  8 BUILDING AND SHARING VALUES

# ROLE PLAYING

### ■ DESCRIPTION

In role playing, two or more individuals act out a brief scenario from a hypothetical situation that the group will then consider through discussion. The "players," usually members of the group, are frequently chosen (or volunteer) because of their spontaneity and flair for drama. The "players" provide an immediate and common experience for the group that can be processed together.

### ■ APPLICATION

This process can be used to explore a potentially troublesome value issue more deeply than traditional methods permit. Participants are psychologically and emotionally drawn into a problem through role play. Role playing can create a group atmosphere of risk-taking and creativity and will often facilitate the sharing of values that need to be encouraged. The "reality practice" aspect of role playing can assist in showing group members how to disagree without being disagreeable, how to tactfully cope with a group member who always monopolizes the conversation, how to give a compliment, or how to accept public praise and recognition gracefully. Value building can occur naturally through drama and humor.

■ **TIME REQUIRED**

Indefinite. Your role playing can be as simple or complex as your "players" want to make it. Don't fall into the trap of losing the focus, however. The crucial part of this process is the discussion that follows.

■ **GROUP SIZE**

Fifteen to thirty-five.

■ **MATERIALS**

The "players" will gather their own props, but these are usually minimal. Arrange the chairs so that everyone can hear clearly, especially if the group is large and the players are not "miked."

■ **PROCESS**

1. State the problem that will be demonstrated in the role play (e.g., members of our staff seem to have little regard for the feelings and personal property of one another).
2. Choose the role players. You may have determined ahead of time who the players will be, or they may be volunteers who are chosen spontaneously.
3. Designate the roles to be played by each player (e.g., the messy teacher, the interruptive teacher, the forgetful teacher, the secretary who usually cleans up after everyone) and set the scene—the teachers' lounge at lunchtime.
4. Give the players time to mentally rehearse their roles.
5. Let the scene unfold.
6. Cut the scene.
7. Allow the actors time to react to the scene they played. Then encourage reaction from the entire audience. Use good discussion methods to focus on a) what actually happened, b) why it happened, and c) suggestions as to how the problem might be solved

Adapted from *Leadership and Dynamic Group Action* by George M. Beal, Joe M. Bohlen, and J. Neil Raudabaugh. Ames, Iowa: The Iowa State University Press, 1962, pp. 251–260.

## PROCESS NUMBER  BUILDING AND SHARING VALUES

# SMALL-GROUP DISCUSSION

■ **DESCRIPTION**

The Small-Group Discussion method is age-old. It has been defined as a "face-to-face mutual interchange of ideas and opinions between members of a relatively small group" (Beal, Bohlen, & Raudabaugh, 1962).

■ **APPLICATION**

This process is best used when the group has an idea, concern, or issue that is worthy of discussion. This process is the "workhorse" of teams and groups and should be used frequently to build relationships and share values.

### ■ TIME REQUIRED
This process can take anywhere from fifteen minutes to one and one half hours. A small-group discussion that lasts longer is usually counterproductive.

### ■ GROUP SIZE
Five to twenty.

### ■ MATERIALS
Chart paper and markers for recording "group memory."

### ■ PROCESS
1. Select a meeting space that will comfortably accommodate the group.
2. Arrange the group in a circle or square so each person can see every other person.
3. Provide table space if possible for the entire group.
4. Appoint a discussion recorder.
5. Take time at appropriate intervals, at least every ten to fifteen minutes, to summarize.
6. As leader, the following behaviors, modeled by you, are critical to the success of small-group discussion:
   - Encourage the free flow of ideas by all team members.
   - Establish an atmosphere that is relaxed, cooperative, and open.
   - Make suggestions rather than giving directives.
   - Use humor where appropriate.
7. Summarize the results of the meeting and ask the recorder to edit and prepare a copy of the discussion notes for the record as soon as possible. If a follow-up meeting is needed, set the time and date.

Adapted from Leadership and Dynamic Group Action by George M. Beal, Joe M. Bohlen, and J. Neil Raudabaugh. Ames, Iowa: The Iowa State University Press, 1962, pp. 181–190.

## PROCESS NUMBER 10  BUILDING AND SHARING VALUES

# THE BUZZ GROUP

### ■ DESCRIPTION
The Buzz Group is a two-person discussion group, which ensures that everyone will participate.

### ■ APPLICATION
Use this process when there is a need to broaden the base of communication and participation, when there is a need for a rapid pooling of ideas from a large

group, and when it is important to create an informal, permissive, and democratic atmosphere. When a small and vociferous minority tries to take control of an issue or discussion, this group process will effectively dilute and even shut down their power.

### ■ TIME REQUIRED
Five or ten minutes.

### ■ GROUP SIZE
Twenty to fifty.

### ■ MATERIALS
A handout of the question under discussion may be needed and cards to record the opinions/findings/ranking of the pairs may also be used, but these are optional.

### ■ PROCESS
1. Count off to form pairs.
2. Give instructions regarding the assignment to be completed in the Buzz Group.
3. Complete assignment and give feedback.

Adapted from Leadership and Dynamic Group Action by George M. Beal, Joe M. Bohlen, and J. Neil Raudabaugh. Ames, Iowa: The Iowa State University Press, 1962, pp. 181-190.

## PROCESS NUMBER 11    BUILDING AND SHARING VALUES

# TURKEY TROT

### ■ DESCRIPTION
The Turkey Trot is a quick way to encourage group members to share compliments and praise with one another.

### ■ APPLICATION
Use this process when group members have begun to take each other for granted and have forgotten the fine art of appreciating one another. This activity is especially timely during the Thanksgiving season.

### ■ TIME REQUIRED
Fifteen minutes.

### ■ GROUP SIZE
Ten to fifty people.

### ■ MATERIALS
Turkeys cut out of brown construction paper for each participant (the turkey outline should be large enough to cover one 8 1/2" × 11" sheet of construction paper). Pens, markers, or pencils.

### PROCESS

1. Hand out one construction-paper turkey to each participant.
2. Instruct participants to write their first and last names in the center of the turkey.
3. Instruct each participant to pass his or her turkey to the left. As each new turkey is received, each participant is to write a compliment, thank-you, or specific word of appreciation to the person whose name is written on the turkey.
4. When all turkeys have been written on by all participants (or when time is called), return the turkeys to their owners.

## PROCESS NUMBER 12 — BUILDING AND SHARING VALUES

# GUESS WHO?

### DESCRIPTION

Guess Who? is an icebreaker to use with a well-established group, particularly a large one that may need some informal interaction together.

### APPLICATION

Use this process when group members have begun to take each other for granted and have forgotten the fine art of appreciating one another.

### TIME REQUIRED

Fifteen minutes.

### GROUP SIZE

Ten to fifty people.

### MATERIALS

One piece of 11" × 14" newsprint or construction paper for each participant. Markers, pencils, or pens. Masking tape.

### PROCESS

1. Tape one piece of paper to the back of each participant.
2. Participants write positive statements about individuals on the pieces of paper taped to each person's back.
3. While participants cannot tell "who" has written "what" about them, there is always some guessing that goes on.
4. After all participants have written their comments (or time is called), each person can remove the sheet and read what has been written.
5. Participants often display the sheets on their bulletin boards.

■ CHAPTER THREE

# Group Processes for Building Teams

---
**HOW DOES A GROUP BECOME A TEAM?**
---
**WHAT ARE THE KEY FACTORS THAT MUST BE PRESENT FOR TEAM DEVELOPMENT TO TAKE PLACE?**
---
**WHAT ROLES MUST BE FULFILLED ON AN EFFECTIVE TEAM?**
---
**WHAT ARE THE EARLY WARNING SIGNALS OF TEAM TROUBLE?**
---
**WHAT PROCESS ACTIVITIES CAN HELP BUILD AN EFFECTIVE TEAM?**
---

## How does a group become a team?

Sports fans are familiar with the team concept. But in sports it's frequently a coach like Bobby Knight or Tom Landry or a star player like Michael Jordan or Joe Montana who get credit for team success. But without the backup of key players and those who play supporting roles, even these stars might shine a little dimmer.

Team building is a process that many leaders take for granted. Eager to move to the agenda (and there is always more to do than we have time for), they bypass the important step of team building. They are rather like classroom teachers, who when first introduced to the concept of cooperative learning, begin using cooperative groups without first taking time to "teach" students how to function in a cooperative group.

The most effective teams have always taken time for team-building activities, and knowledgeable team leaders are always sensitive to the need for periodic "time-outs" from task-oriented activities to assess the progress of the team in critical areas such as communication, conflict management, cohesiveness, role clarity, and sense of purpose. Sports teams are frequently said to be rebuilding. They have added new members and are working not only to teach new plays, but to build team spirit.

Teams do not just happen. They are rather like growing children who go through stages or phases. Knowledge of these stages can help the leader to prescribe activities to encourage team building at various points in the team's life, and an awareness of the stages can also console the leader when those bleak moments of total dysfunction temporarily paralyze even the most effective teams.

> A group of people is not a team. A team is a group of people with a high degree of interdependence geared toward the achievement of a goal or completion of a task. In other words, they agree on a goal and agree that the only way to achieve the goal is to work together.
> —Glenn M. Parker

There are a variety of ways to characterize the stages of team development.

One author labels the stages Getting Started, Going in Circles, Getting on Course, and Full Speed Ahead.[1] Another popular model is the one I've always called the "ing" model: Forming, Storming, Norming, and Performing.[2] My preferred model of team development, however, is the one suggested by Lynch and Werner: Formation, Familiarity, Power, Performance, and Synergy.[3]

In each stage of team development, there are key responsibilities that must be carried out by both the leader and the team members.[4] Failure on the part of either to accept and fulfill these responsibilities will result in a dysfunctional team. In the Formation Stage, there are many start-up tasks to complete—developing a team mission, creating team traditions, and accepting the new team identity. Team members in this stage are not yet ready to take risks or share information about themselves, and some may even have old biases and grudges that keep them from letting go of the past. In the second stage, Familiarity, members must begin to get to know each other, appreciate one another, and open themselves up to risks. In the Power Stage, team members should begin to show their colors, do some healthy disagreeing, even rebel against the team leader. If a team can't resolve these conflicts productively, it will not survive. The Performance Stage will see the team working together effectively, a well-oiled machine that is successfully solving problems and making decisions. Most teams feel fortunate if they reach this stage. Many

> To lead change, you have to change.
> —Robert F. Lynch and Thomas J. Werner

never do. They muddle around in the power stage, bogged down by politics and an unwillingness to open up, let go, and join in. So it is the rare team that makes it to the

Synergy Stage. These teams are the ones that win world championships. They show a "high degree of unity and commitment to the team's mission; the members are energetic and enthusiastic; and the members will often sacrifice for the sake of the team's performance."[5]

## What are the key factors that must be present for team development to take place?

I've often fantasized about putting a small group of individuals in a room and giving them the instructions: "Don't come out until you're a team." I, of course, as the team leader, would not be present for this shoot-out. But without the following key attributes, however, they might never make it:

- Commitment (a willingness to put group goals above personal goals)
- Trust (a feeling of confidence and support on the part of group members for each other)
- Purpose (understanding of what the team's mission is)
- Communication (the ability to handle conflict, decision making, and day-to-day interaction)
- Involvement (partnership and ownership in the team's mission)
- Process orientation (tools, activities, processes, structures for dealing with the day-to-day operation of the team)[6]

And what if your team doesn't have these characteristics? What then? It is your responsibility as the leader to "build that team." With some groups you may need to begin with new blueprints. Bring in an architect (such as a consultant) to help you re-draw them. With other groups, team building may mean only a little refurbishing here and there. Some teams you will lead are newly formed; others are already established and you have been hired as their new leader; and in still other cases, new members may join an already-established team. In each case, the needs of the team will be different. Be sensitive to the kinds of team-building activities your team needs.

## What roles must be fulfilled on an effective team?

There are a variety of roles that must be fulfilled in order for a group to function as an effective team. Ideally, as teams are constituted or new members are chosen to fill vacancies on an already-existing team, the styles and personalities of group members will be considered. There are four types or styles of team players and all are needed. Still, these same personalities, if carried to the extreme, can prove to be the undoing of a team. These are the four:[7] Contributor, Collaborator,

| Contributor | | Collaborator | |
|---|---|---|---|
| **POSITIVE TRAITS** | **NEGATIVE TRAITS** | **POSITIVE TRAITS** | **NEGATIVE TRAITS** |
| • dependable | • compulsive | • cooperative | • overcommitted |
| • efficient | • perfectionistic | • conceptual | • insensitive |
| • logical | • uncreative | • visionary | • overinvolved |
| • pragmatic | • data-bound | • flexible | • too global |
| • systematic | | • imaginative | |

| Communicator | | Challenger | |
|---|---|---|---|
| **POSITIVE TRAITS** | **NEGATIVE TRAITS** | **POSITIVE TRAITS** | **NEGATIVE TRAITS** |
| • supportive | • aimless | • candid | • rigid |
| • encouraging | • foolish | • ethical | • arrogant |
| • relaxed | • placating | • outspoken | • self-righteous |
| • helpful | • manipulative | • adventurous | • contentious |
| • considerate | | • principled | • nit-picking |
| • patient | | | |

Communicator, and Challenger. Each has a role to play, sometimes positive, sometimes negative. Your job is to bring out the best in everyone. The positive Contributor is dependable, efficient, logical, pragmatic, and systematic. The negative Contributor is compulsive, perfectionistic, uncreative, and data-bound. The positive Collaborator is cooperative, conceptual, visionary, flexible, and imaginative. The negative Collaborator is overcommitted, insensitive, overinvolved, and too global. The positive Communicator is supportive, encouraging, relaxed, helpful, considerate, and patient. The negative Communicator is aimless, foolish, placating, and manipulative. The positive Challenger is candid, ethical, outspoken, adventurous, and principled. The negative Challenger is rigid, arrogant, self-righteous, contentious, and nit-picking.[8]

And what happens when the leader's role is filled with a Collaborator, a Communicator, a Challenger, or a Contributor? How will that change the dynamics of the group's effectiveness?

In a fully functional and effective team, all of the roles must be filled. If you tend more toward only one of the styles, rather than being a composite as many effective leaders are, you will need to make sure that your team members understand and recognize your style and are able to complement it and compensate for its drawbacks.

If you are a Contributor Leader, you will focus on the efficient operation of your team. You will make sure that problems are solved and that work moves along according to strict timelines. If you are a Collaborator Leader, you will excel at providing the visionary and strategic thinking necessary for solving the problems of the future. If you are a Communicator Leader, you will be comfortable with participatory and shared decision making. And finally, if you are a Challenger Leader, you will excel at establishing openness and candor in your group.[9]

> A team is an energetic group of people who are committed to achieving common objectives, who work well together and enjoy doing so, and produce high quality results.
>
> —Dave Francis and Don Young

## What are the early warning signals of team trouble?

Attend any team meeting as a first-time visitor (as I often have), and almost immediately one can sense if there are early warning signs of team trouble as described by G. M. Parker in *Team Players and Teamwork.* (1990):

- Team members can't easily describe or agree on the team's mission.
- Meetings are formal, stuffy, or tense.
- Broad participation produces minimal accomplishment.
- There is talk, but not much communication.
- Team members air disagreements privately after meetings.
- The formal leader makes all the decisions.
- Members are confused or disagree about role or work assignments.
- Key people outside the team aren't cooperating.
- The team leader has all of the responsibility for meeting team needs; team members do not handle any team functions.
- The team has not assessed its progress and process.[10]

## What process activities can help build an effective team?

The following process activities are designed to build a team with the members of your group. Some are very simple and can be completed in a short time. Some are assessment instruments to help you and your team members determine which specific aspects of the team process need special attention. Other processes are designed to take several hours, and while the content may be unrelated to the mission of your team, the experiences may create epiphanies of sorts for team members as they realize the power of being a team.

Each process has six parts: 1. Description, 2. Application, 3. Time Required, 4. Group Size, 5. Materials, and 6. Process.

**PROCESS NUMBER 1  TEAM BUILDING**

## BROKEN SQUARES

### ■ DESCRIPTION

Broken Squares is a process through which group participants learn about the value of cooperation in solving a group problem and are sensitized to some of their own behaviors that may contribute to or obstruct the solving of a group problem.

### ■ APPLICATION

Use this process with a team that has not yet learned the value of cooperation and whose members do not fully appreciate the gifts and talents of fellow group members. Use the process to build a spirit of teamwork and cooperation.

### ■ TIME REQUIRED

Fifteen minutes for the exercise and fifteen minutes for discussion.

### ■ GROUP SIZE

Any number of groups of six participants each. There will be five active participants and an observer/judge. A minimum of six participants is needed, but eighteen is better.

### ■ MATERIALS

Chalkboard, chalk, eraser. Tables to seat five participants. One set of instructions for each group of five and one for the observer/judge. One set of broken squares for each group of five participants.

### ■ PROCESS

1. Begin with a discussion of the meaning of cooperation. Elicit some suggestions

from the group regarding the essential elements of cooperation in solving a problem.

2. Inform the group that it will be conducting an experiment to test the validity of members' suggestions. If the group has not brought forth the following suggestions as essential elements, include them in the discussion:
   - Each individual must understand the total problem.
   - Each individual should understand how he or she can contribute toward solving the problem.
   - Each individual should be aware of the potential contributions of other individuals.
   - There is a need to recognize the problems of other individuals, in order to aid them in making their maximum contribution.

3. Divide the group into teams of six. Select an observer/judge for each group. The observers/judges are responsible for making notes about behaviors they see, both positive and counterproductive, that occur during the solution of the problem. Distribute the envelopes from the prepared packets (See Directions for Making a Set of Squares). The envelopes are to remain unopened until the signal to work is given.

4. Distribute a copy of the instructions to each group (See Participant Instructions).

5. Read the instructions to the group, calling for questions as you go. Monitor the tables during the exercise to enforce the rules that have been established in the instructions.

6. When all the groups have completed the task, engage the groups in a discussion of the experience. Discussion should focus on feelings more than merely relating experiences and general observations. Observations should also be solicited from the observers/judges. Draw conclusions about the relevance of this exercise to "real life" situations.

The following resources were used for this process: Alex Bavelas, "Communication Patterns in Task-Oriented Groups," *Journal of the Acoustical Society of America*, Vol. 22 (1950): 725–730; notes a from lecture by Dr. Nicholas DeLuca, Department of Educational Administration, Northern Illinois University, May 1979; and Ronald T. Hyman, *School Administrator's Staff Development Activities Manual*, Englewood Cliffs, New Jersey: Prentice Hall, Inc., 1986.

# DIRECTIONS FOR MAKING A SET OF SQUARES

A set of squares consists of five envelopes, each containing pieces of cardboard that have been cut into different patterns and that, when properly arranged, will form five squares of equal size. One set should be provided for each group of five persons.

To prepare a set, cut out five cardboard squares of equal size, approximately 6 x 6 inches. Place the squares in a row and mark them as below, penciling the letters a,b,c, etc., lightly so that they can later be erased.

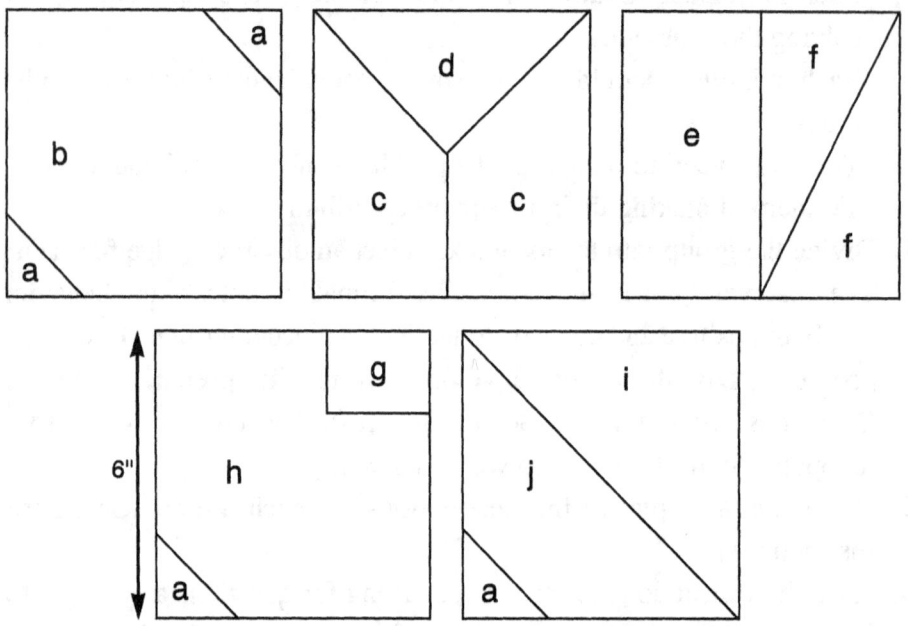

The lines should be so drawn that, when cut out, all pieces marked "a" will be exactly the same size, all pieces marked "c" the same size, etc. By using multiples of three inches, several combinations will be possible that will enable participants to form one or two squares, but only one combination is possible that will form five squares 6 x 6 inches.

After drawing the lines on the 6 x 6-inch squares and labeling them with lowercase letters, cut each square as marked into smaller pieces to make the parts of the puzzle.

Mark the five envelopes A, B, C, D, and E. Distribute the cardboard pieces in the five envelopes as follows:

    Envelope A has pieces i, h, and e.

    Envelope B has pieces a, a, a, and one c.

    Envelope C has pieces a and j.

    Envelope D has pieces d and one f.

    Envelope E has pieces g, b, f, and one c.

Erase the penciled letter from each piece and write, instead, the appropriate envelope letter. This will make it easy to return the pieces to the proper envelopes for subsequent use when a group has completed the task.

SOURCE: From Bavelas, A., "Communication Patterns in Task-Oriented Groups." *Journal of the Acoustical Society of America*, 22, 725-730. Copyright © 1950. Reprinted by permission.

## PARTICIPANT INSTRUCTIONS

Distributed among you are envelopes containing pieces of a puzzle. Each group has its own complete set of five envelopes. These pieces will form five complete squares of equal dimensions with one of them to be placed in front of each member of your group. That is, each square will be the same size as each of the other four. Your task is to assemble a square in front of you. Each person is to assemble one square in front of him or her. You must observe these rules:

1. You may not ask for a piece from someone else in your group. This includes asking in any way, verbally or nonverbally. You may not signal, gesture, motion, take a piece, or in any other way try to get a piece from someone else in your group.
2. You may get a piece from someone else only if that person gives it to you.
3. If you give a piece to another person, you may not put it in place for him or her. You may only give someone else a piece and then that person must position that piece him- or herself.
4. You may give any of your pieces to any other group member. You may give away at any time all of your pieces, if you so wish. If you give away all of your pieces, you must do so one piece at a time; you may not give away your pieces assembled.
5. You may not talk at any time during this activity. The observers/judges will help enforce these rules.

SOURCE: From Bavelas, A., "Communication Patterns in Task-Oriented Groups." *Journal of the Acoustical Society of America*, 22, 725-730. Copyright © 1950. Reprinted by permission.

# PROCESS NUMBER 2  TEAM BUILDING

# LOST ON THE MOON

## ■ DESCRIPTION

Lost on the Moon is a process in which participants imagine themselves to be members of a space crew who have crash-landed on the moon hundreds of miles away from their mother ship. They must decide which items of the fifteen left intact after the crash are the most important for survival.

## ■ APPLICATION

This process gives participants a chance to "practice" consensual decision making around a problem that is neutral. When a team does not understand the consensus decision-making process or team members need to learn to value the worth of each team member, this process can be very helpful.

## ■ TIME REQUIRED

Forty-five minutes for groups to rank order their choices. Thirty to forty-five minutes for debriefing.

## ■ GROUP SIZE

Four groups of five members each is ideal. Fewer participants will diminish the power of the discussion.

## ■ MATERIALS

A copy of the Lost on the Moon Instructions for each participant, a copy of Instructions for Consensus for each participant, and a scoring sheet for each group.

## ■ PROCESS

1. Give each participant a copy of the Lost on the Moon Instructions.
2. Read through the directions aloud. Allow five minutes for the participants to rank the items.
3. Give each participant a copy of the Instructions for Consensus.
4. Read through the directions aloud as needed.
5. Give each participant a copy of the scoring sheet. Give groups about forty-five minutes to reach consensus about their rank orderings and then ask them to tabulate the results. In each group let one person act as recorder while each group member calls out his private rank orderings of the fifteen items. The recorder will then sum the ranking for each of the items and rank order the sums, thus arriving at an average rank order for the group. (This represents

the rank order that might have been obtained had the group merely voted and not held a discussion). The recorder also records the rank order that the group has reached by consensus.

6. Distribute the rank ordering given by NASA (the correct answer). Ask the recorders to record this information on their sheets as well. Each recorder should then compute three scores by summing the arithmetic discrepancies between the correct rank order and the rank order obtained through consensus, the average rank order of the group before discussion, and the individual rank order that came closest to the NASA rank order.

7. Each group should then determine whether its "best" individual score, the group's average score produced before discussion, or its consensual score, is best.

8. After group members have informally discussed their scores, the group discussion should focus on these three questions:
   - What were my reactions to the exercise? How did I feel? What was I thinking?
   - How similar were our behaviors here to our usual behaviors in our team meetings? How different? What are the implications of this exercise for the productivity of our team?
   - How well did we use our group resources? What kept us from being more productive? How could the obstacles we encountered have been avoided?

The following resources were used for this process: Jay Hall, "Decisions, Decisions, Decisions," *Psychology Today* 5:51–54, 86, 88, 1971; Richard A. Schmuck, Philip J. Runkel, Jane H. Arends, and Richard I. Arends, *The Second Handbook of Organization Development in Schools;* and notes from a lecture by Dr. Nicholas DeLuca, Department of Educational Administration, Northern Illinois University, May 1979.

## LOST ON THE MOON INSTRUCTIONS

Instructions: You are a member of a space crew originally scheduled to rendezvous with a mother ship on the lighted surface of the moon. Because of mechanical difficulties, however, your ship has been forced to land at a spot some 200 miles from the rendezvous point. During the rough landing, much of the equipment aboard was damaged, and, since survival depends on reaching the mother ship, only the most critical items aboard must be chosen for the 200-mile trip. Below are listed the fifteen items left intact and undamaged after landing. Your task is to rank order them in terms of their importance in enabling your crew to reach the rendezvous point. Place the number 1 by the most important item, the number 2 by the second most important, and so on through number 15, the least important.

_____ Solar-powered radio FM receiver/transmitter

_____ Food concentrate

_____ Fifty feet of nylon rope

_____ Box of matches

_____ Parachute silk

_____ Solar-powered portable heating unit

_____ Two .45 calibre pistols

_____ One case dehydrated Pet milk

_____ Two 100-lb. tanks of oxygen

_____ Stellar map of moon's constellations

_____ Self-inflating life raft

_____ Magnetic compass

_____ Five gallons of water

_____ Signal flares

_____ First-aid kit containing injection needles

SOURCE: Reprinted from *The Second Handbook of Organization Development in Schools* by Richard A. Schmuck, Philip J. Runkel, Jane H. Arends, and Richard I. Arends, Center for Educational Policy and Management, University of Oregon, 1977.

# INSTRUCTIONS FOR CONSENSUS

Consensus is a decision process for making full use of resources and for resolving conflicts creatively. Consensus is difficult to reach, so not every ranking will meet with everyone's complete approval. Complete unanimity is not the goal—it is rarely achieved. But each individual should be able to accept the group rankings on the basis of logic and feasibility. When all group members feel able to accept a particular ranking, you have reached consensus as defined here, and the judgment may be entered as a group decision. This means, in effect, that a person can block the group if he thinks it is necessary; at the same time, he should use this option in the best sense of reciprocity. Here are some guidelines to use in achieving consensus.

1. Avoid arguing for your own rankings. Present your position as lucidly and logically as possible, but listen to the other members' reactions and consider them carefully before you press your point.

2. Do not assume that someone must win and someone must lose when discussion reaches a stalemate. Instead, look for the next most acceptable alternative for all parties.

3. Do not change your mind simply to avoid conflict and to reach agreement and harmony. When agreement seems to come too quickly and easily, be suspicious. Explore the reasons for agreement and be sure everyone accepts the solution for basically similar or complementary reasons. Yield only to positions that have objective and logical foundations.

4. Avoid conflict-reducing techniques such as majority vote, averages, coin flips, and bargaining. When a dissenting member finally agrees, don't feel that this person must be rewarded by having his or her own way on some later point.

5. Differences of opinion are natural and expected. Seek them out and try to involve everyone in the decision process. Disagreements can help the group's decision because, with a wide range of information and opinions, there is a greater chance that the group will find a better solution.

SOURCE: Reprinted from *The Second Handbook of Organization Development in Schools* by Richard A. Schmuck, Philip J. Runkel, Jane H. Arends, and Richard I. Arends, Center for Educational Policy and Management, University of Oregon, 1977.

## NASA RANKINGS

___5___ Solar-powered radio FM receiver/transmitter

___4___ Food concentrate

___6___ Fifty feet of nylon rope

___15___ Box of matches

___8___ Parachute silk

___13___ Solar-powered portable heating unit

___11___ Two .45 calibre pistols

___12___ One case dehydrated Pet milk

___1___ Two 100-lb. tanks of oxygen

___3___ Stellar map of moon's constellations

___9___ Self-inflating life raft

___14___ Magnetic compass

___2___ Five gallons of water

___10___ Signal flares

___7___ First-aid kit containing injection needles

SOURCE: Reprinted from *The Second Handbook of Organization Development in Schools* by Richard A. Schmuck, Philip J. Runkel, Jane H. Arends, and Richard I. Arends, Center for Educational Policy and Management, University of Oregon, 1977.

# LOST ON THE MOON SCORING SHEET

| Scoring Sheet for Lost on the Moon | Individual Rankings | | | | | | | | | | Sums of ind. ranks | Ranking of sums | Consensual Ranking | NASA's Ranking |
|---|---|---|---|---|---|---|---|---|---|---|---|---|---|---|
| | 1 | 2 | 3 | 4 | 5 | 6 | 7 | 8 | 9 | 10 | | | | |
| Solar-powered radio FM receiver/transmitter | | | | | | | | | | | | | | |
| Food concentrate | | | | | | | | | | | | | | |
| 50 feet of nylon rope | | | | | | | | | | | | | | |
| Box of matches | | | | | | | | | | | | | | |
| Parachute silk | | | | | | | | | | | | | | |
| Solar-powered portable heating unit | | | | | | | | | | | | | | |
| Two .45 calibre pistols | | | | | | | | | | | | | | |
| One case dehydrated Pet milk | | | | | | | | | | | | | | |
| Two 100-lb. tanks of oxygen | | | | | | | | | | | | | | |
| Stellar map of moon's constellations | | | | | | | | | | | | | | |
| Self-inflating life raft | | | | | | | | | | | | | | |
| Magnetic compass | | | | | | | | | | | | | | |
| Five gallons of water | | | | | | | | | | | | | | |
| Signal flares | | | | | | | | | | | | | | |
| First-aid kit containing injection needles | | | | | | | | | | | | | | |

SOURCE: Reprinted from *The Second Handbook of Organization Development in Schools* by Richard A. Schmuck, Philip J. Runkel, Jane H. Arends, and Richard I. Arends, Center for Educational Policy and Management, University of Oregon, 1977.

**PROCESS NUMBER 3  TEAM BUILDING**

# HOLLOW SQUARE PATTERN

## ■ DESCRIPTION

This process requires that a planning team decide how to solve a problem and then give instructions to an operating team for implementation. The problem consists of assembling sixteen pieces of cardboard into the form of a hollow square. The planning team is supplied with the general layout of the pieces. This team is not to assemble the parts itself, but is to instruct the operating team on how to assemble the parts in a minimum amount of time.

## ■ APPLICATION

This process demonstrates to group members that it is far easier to plan than it is to implement. This process should be used with well-established groups because it is a high-risk activity and participants may well get agitated about their ability (or lack thereof) to perform under pressure.

## ■ TIME REQUIRED

One hour.

## ■ GROUP SIZE

Four-member operating team; four-member planning team; and an observation team of from four to ten members.

## ■ MATERIALS

Copy of Hollow Square Operating Team Briefing Sheet for each observation team member. Copy of Hollow Square Planning Team Briefing Sheet for each planning team member. Copy of Hollow Square Observing Team Briefing Sheet for each operating team member. Four packets for each of the planning team members, containing the sixteen cardboard pieces that will form the Hollow Square when assembled (to be prepared by the facilitator using the Hollow Square Key). A copy of the Hollow Square Key and the Hollow Square Pattern for each planning team.

## ■ PROCESS

1. Divide the large group into operating team(s), planning team(s), and observation team(s).
2. Pass out applicable materials to each group.
3. Review instructions with each group.
4. During the twenty-five minutes in which the planning team is completing their assignment, monitor the discussion and activities of the two other groups.
5. Assemble the teams for the activity.

6. Debrief by discussing strengths and weaknesses of the planning team's work. Solicit feedback from the observers relative to what happened during the process. Solicit input from the implementation team relative to their successes/failures. Ask them to give feedback to the planning team relative to the clarity and simplicity of their instructions.

Adapted from the lecture and notes of Dr. Nicholas DeLuca, Professor of Educational Administration,<br>Northern Illinois University, May 1980.

---

### HOLLOW SQUARE OPERATING TEAM BRIEFING SHEET

1. You will have responsibility for carrying out a task for four people according to instructions given by your planning team. Your planning team may call you in for instructions at any time. If they do not summon you, you are to report to them anyway. Your task is scheduled to begin exactly twenty-five minutes from now. After that, no further instructions will be permitted.

2. You are to finish the assigned task as rapidly as possible.

3. During the period when you are waiting for a call from your planning team, it is suggested that you discuss and make notes on the following questions:

    - What feelings and concerns do you experience while waiting for instructions for the unknown task?
    - How can the four of you organize as a team?

4. The notes recorded on the above will be helpful during the discussion following the completion of the task.

---

SOURCE: Handout provided during lecture by Dr. Nicholas DeLuca,<br>Professor of Educational Administration, Northern Illinois University, May 1980.

## HOLLOW SQUARE PLANNING TEAM BRIEFING SHEET

Each of you will be given a packet containing four cardboard pieces that, when properly assembled with the other pieces held by members of your team, will make a hollow square design.

Your Task:

During a period of twenty-five minutes you are to do the following:

1. Plan how the sixteen pieces distributed among you should be assembled to make the design.

2. Instruct your operating team on how to implement your plan. (You may begin instructing your operating team at any time during the planning period, but no later than five minutes before they are to begin the assembling process.)

General Rules:

1. You must keep all pieces that you have in front of you at all times.

2. You may not touch or trade pieces with other members of your team during the planning or instructing phase.

3. You may not show the Key at any time.

4. You may not assemble the entire square at any time (this is to be left to your operating team).

5. You are not to mark on any of the pieces.

6. Members of your operating team must also observe the same rules.

7. When time is called for your team to give the pieces to the operating team, you may give no further instruction, but you are to observe the operation.

SOURCE: Handout provided during lecture by Dr. Nicholas DeLuca, Professor of Educational Administration, Northern Illinois University, May 1980.

# HOLLOW SQUARE OBSERVING TEAM BRIEFING SHEET

You will be observing a situation in which a planning team decides how to solve a problem and gives instructions to an operating team for implementation. The problem consists of assembling sixteen pieces of cardboard into the form of a hollow square. The planning team is supplied with the general layout of the pieces. This team is not to assemble the parts itself, but is to instruct the operating team on how to assemble the parts in a minimum amount of time. You will be silent observers throughout the process.

Suggestions:

1. Each member of the observing team should watch the general pattern of communication but give special attention to one member of the planning team (during the planning phase) and one member of the operating team (during the assembling period).

2. During the planning period watch for the following:
   - Is there balanced participation among planning team members?
   - How were decisions made?
   - Which decision style predominated?
   - Did everyone agree?
   - Which mechanism/media were chosen to transmit decisions?
   - How did the planning team use its time? What activities did they engage in?

3. During the instruction period watch for the following behaviors:
   - Which member of the planning team gives the instructions? How was this decided?
   - What strategy was employed in orienting the operating team to the task?
   - What assumptions made by the planning team were not communicated to the operating team?
   - How effective were the instructions?
   - Did the operating team appear to feel free to ask questions of the planners?

4. During the assembly period watch for the following:
   - What evidence is there that the operating team members understood or misunderstood the instructions?
   - Were all the decisions made by the planning committee carried out as intended?
   - Were there any decisions that clearly facilitated or clearly hindered the assembly process?

SOURCE: Handout provided during lecture by Dr. Nicholas DeLuca, Professor of Educational Administration, Northern Illinois University, May 1980.

# HOLLOW SQUARE KEY

(not drawn to scale)

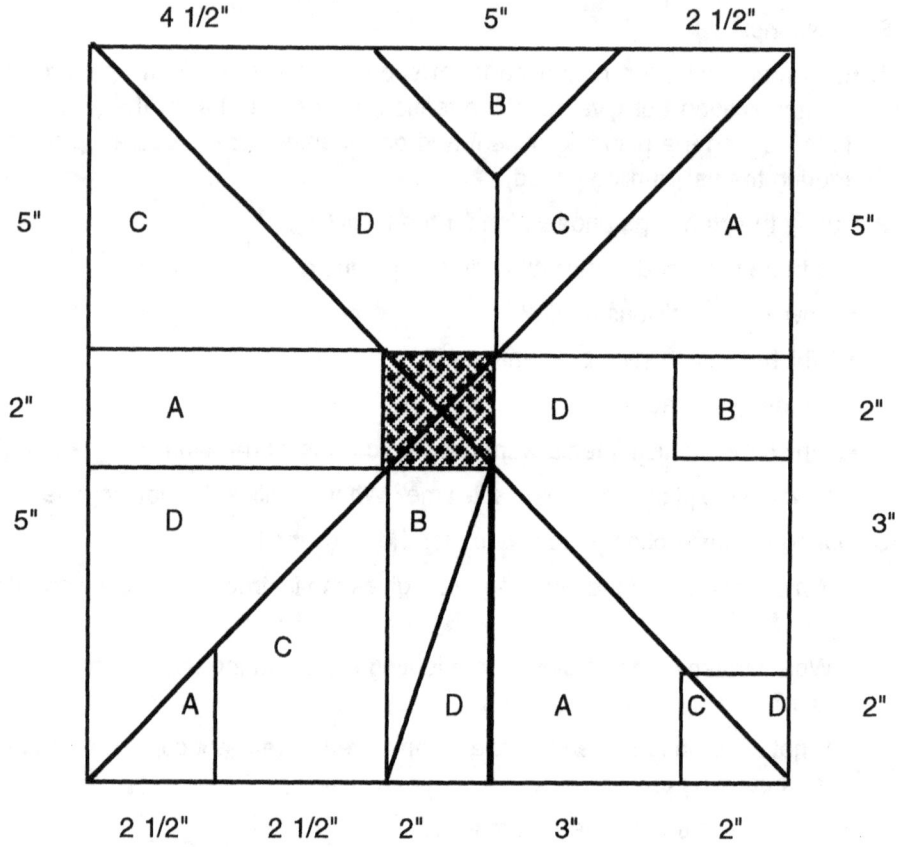

To Facilitator: Construct a hollow square from cardboard or heavy paper using the above key. Place all A pieces in one envelope, all B pieces in a second envelope, etc. Do not label the individual pieces. The square when assembled should measure 12" × 12".

SOURCE: Handout provided during lecture by Dr. Nicholas DeLuca, Professor of Educational Administration, Northern Illinois University, May 1980.

# HOLLOW SQUARE PATTERN

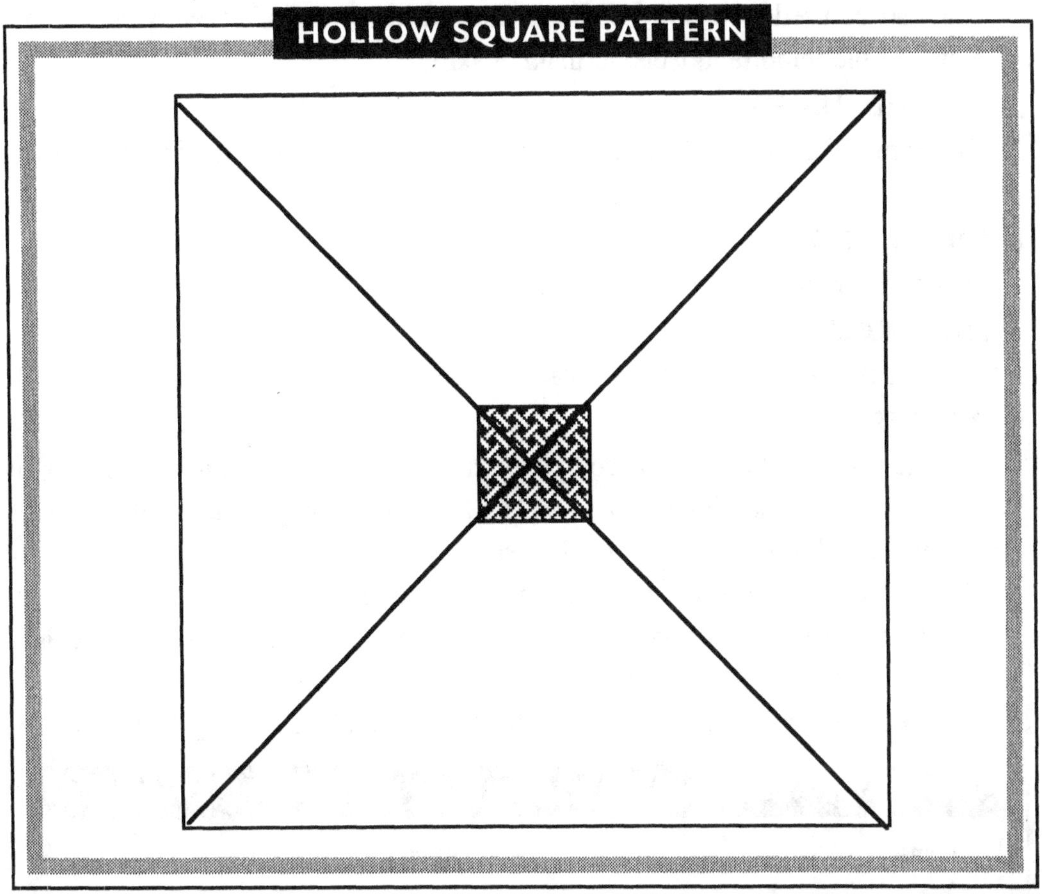

SOURCE: Handout provided during lecture by Dr. Nicholas DeLuca, Professor of Educational Administration, Northern Illinois University, May 1980.

## PROCESS NUMBER 4 — TEAM BUILDING

# INDIVIDUAL AND GROUP ASSESSMENT OF DECISION-MAKING SKILLS

### ■ DESCRIPTION

This process is an assessment instrument to help participants gain a clear picture of each subset of skills needed by individuals and groups for quality decision making. Each subset of skills is covered in its own chapter; this chapter focuses on team building. Participants can rate their own behaviors when working as a team member, the functioning of the team as a whole, or both.

### ■ APPLICATION

When a team has been working together for a period of time and is experiencing difficulties in communication, conflict resolution, or creative problem solving, this instrument will determine exactly where the problem lies. The instrument can also be used as a staff development tool to give a quick overview to new teams of the important decision-making skills.

## ■ TIME REQUIRED

Thirty minutes to complete the questionnaire and thirty to forty-five minutes to discuss and process the results.

## ■ GROUP SIZE

Any team from five to twenty members.

## ■ MATERIALS

Copy of the assessment for each participant.

## ■ PROCESS

1. After each participant has completed his or her questionnaire, a secretary or other neutral individual should collate the results and present them in an easily readable form to the group leader.
2. The group leader should present the results to the group.
3. What specific actions will the team need to take immediately to improve their individual or group behavior?
4. Select two to four skills on which the team will focus for improvement.

---

### INDIVIDUAL AND GROUP ASSESSMENT OF DECISION-MAKING SKILLS

Name _____ Group Name _____

**Directions for Individual Assessment**
Examine the behaviors you exhibit while working as a member of your team. On a 5-point scale (1 = I never do; 5 = I always do), rate yourself on the following decision-making skills. Place a check mark next to the 2 to 4 skills on which you personally wish to focus.

**Directions for Group Assessment**
Reflect on your team's decision-making skills. On a 5-point scale (1= We never do; 5= We always do), rate your entire team. Compare your total team rating with those of your teammates and together select 2 to 4 skills on which the team will work.

**Building and Sharing Values**

| SELF | | GROUP |
|---|---|---|
| _____ | I/we can articulate the values that are most important to our team, school, or organization. | _____ |
| _____ | I/we have a sense of the shared history and tradition of which we are a part. | _____ |
| _____ | I/we know important things about each other, both personal and professional. | _____ |
| _____ | I/we are committed to a set of core values that guide our behaviors and decision making. | _____ |

## Team Building

SELF                                                                                               GROUP

_____ I/we have a willingness to put group goals above personal ones. _____

_____ I/we have a sense of trust and confidence in fellow team members. _____

_____ I/we understand and believe in the team's mission. _____

_____ I/we have the ability to communicate with one another on a variety of issues and levels. _____

_____ I/we volunteer for roles that help to maintain a harmonious working group (e.g., encourage everyone to participate). _____

_____ I/we feel a sense of partnership and ownership in the team's mission. _____

## Generating Ideas

SELF                                                                                               GROUP

_____ I/we can listen to what others are saying with an open mind. _____

_____ I/we are able to use a variety of approaches to creativity (e.g., visual, verbal). _____

_____ I/we are able to generate as many reasons why something will work as reasons why it won't. _____

_____ I/we can explain, clarify, or ask for help. _____

_____ I/we can motivate the team by using humor or enthusiasm when interest is flagging. _____

_____ I/we can appreciate a variety of thinking and learning styles. _____

## Sharing Critical Information

SELF                                                                                               GROUP

_____ I/we can articulate ideas and information in a way that can be understood by others. _____

_____ I/we are able to learn and hear a variety of points of view before moving to decision making. _____

_____ I/we can explore many facets of a complex issue and ask thoughtful questions. _____

_____ I/we can engage in a meaningful dialogue with another person who may have a different point of view than I/we hold. _____

## Problem Solving

SELF                                                                                               GROUP

_____ I/we are willing to face problems whether they are analytical, creative, or judgmental in nature. _____

_____ I/we are willing to face problems as they occur. _____

_____ I/we are willing to share our ideas and solutions in a public forum and accept the suggestions or instructive criticism of others. _____

_____ I/we are willing to face weaknesses in our team or organization on the way to identifying strengths and solving problems. _____

## Reaching Consensus

SELF                                                                                  GROUP

_____ I/we have a level of trust that allows honesty, directness, and candor.

_____ I/we have a healthy interaction style that allows for open disagreement and does not facilitate or condone dominating and manipulating behaviors.

_____ I/we can tolerate conflict, ambiguity, controversy, temporary stalemates, and shifts of opinion.

_____ I/we keep well informed about critical issues in order to participate in the process intelligently.

## Resolving Conflict

SELF                                                                                  GROUP

_____ I/we believe that conflicts can be resolved.

_____ I/we believe that resolving conflicts is a worthy goal.

_____ I/we believe in cooperation rather than competition.

_____ I/we believe that everyone on the team is of equal value.

_____ I/we believe that other team members' statements are accurate views of their positions and that they have a right to change those views in the course of a discussion.

_____ I/we believe that differences of opinion are helpful.

_____ I/we believe that fellow team members are trustworthy.

_____ I/we can critique ideas without criticizing those who hold the ideas.

_____ I/we can see an issue from several different points of view.

_____ I/we can request that others offer justification and supporting evidence for their viewpoints.

## Goal Setting and Planning

SELF                                                                                  GROUP

_____ I/we can determine which of the many worthwhile goals that might be accomplished should be targeted.

_____ I/we can be realistic in selecting goals.

_____ I/we can be flexible in changing plans when the need for reversal is necessary.

_____ I/we can divide a large task into many smaller steps.

_____ I/we can develop time schedules for completion of key tasks.

_____ I/we can identify subgoals of a larger mission or vision.

_____ I/we can procure the resources necessary to reach our goals.

**PROCESS NUMBER 5  TEAM BUILDING**

# WHAT'S OUR TEAMING QUOTIENT?

## ■ DESCRIPTION

This process is an easy-to-complete checklist that asks team members to rate the effectiveness of the team and its meetings.

## ■ APPLICATION

Use this questionnaire when a well-established team is experiencing difficulties making quality decisions. Use of the questionnaire will permit the group to deal with problem issues in a structured way and allow serious team problems to be addressed. This process could be used in training new teams to introduce them to the important aspects of an effective team.

## ■ TIME REQUIRED

Fifteen minutes for the completion of the questionnaire and thirty minutes to process the results.

## ■ GROUP SIZE

Ten to twenty participants.

## ■ MATERIALS

Copy of the questionnaire for each participant.

## ■ PROCESS

1. Pass out a copy of the questionnaire to each participant.
2. When each participant has completed his or her individual answers, collect the questionnaires and have the group secretary tally the results. If all group members answer yes to an item, the team receives the number of points to the right of the item. Total the number of points circled for the team. The maximum score is 100.
3. Compare your team score to the Scoring Guide to receive an overall rating.
4. Determine which items received the most "no" answers and determine what can be done to improve the team score.

## WHAT'S OUR TEAMING QUOTIENT?

Circle yes or no for each statement below as it applies to your team. The point total to the right of each item will be assigned to your team if every team member answers yes to that question. The maximum score any team can receive is 100.

**POINTS**

1. Our team meets in an environment that is well appointed and comfortable. YES NO 2
2. Our team meetings begin promptly. YES NO 2
3. Team members can see and hear every other member of the team during the meetings. YES NO 2
4. All team members have the opportunity to ask questions and share ideas. YES NO 3
5. All team members:
   - attend meetings unless ill or out of town. YES NO 2
   - arrive on time. YES NO 2
   - stay for the entire meeting. YES NO 2
   - actively participate in the discussion and decision making. YES NO 3
   - actively assume responsibility for tasks that need to be accomplished YES NO 3
6. Our team has regularly scheduled meetings that are held at times and places agreed on in advance. YES NO 2
7. Tardy team members are updated during a break or following the meeting. YES NO 2
8. Absent team members are notified of critical information. YES NO 2
9. Our meeting agendas are planned to insure that our team:
   - identifies agenda items for the next meeting before adjourning the current meeting. YES NO 2
   - reviews action items from previous meetings. YES NO 2
   - establishes time limits for each agenda item. YES NO 2
   - creates minutes that are available to all team members in advance of team meetings. YES NO 2
   - debriefs on group effectiveness regarding task accomplishment and interpersonal skills. YES NO 3
   - reviews and modifies the agenda, when necessary. YES NO 2
   - reviews the group memory of what was decided and who is responsible for action items. YES NO 2
   - distributes the homework and action items fairly among team members. YES NO 2
   - generally accomplishes the tasks on the agenda. YES NO 3
   - adjourns meetings on time. YES NO 2

| | | | |
|---|---|---|---|
| 10. Our team has a published mission statement. | YES | NO | 3 |
| 11. We have established group social norms that are shared with new team members through a formal initiation or training session (e.g., no gossiping, no put-downs). | YES | NO | 3 |
| 12. Our team takes mutual responsibility for failure and never points fingers or lays blame on individual team members. | YES | NO | 3 |
| 13. Team members are free to express feelings (both negative and positive). | YES | NO | 3 |
| 14. Our team has systems in place for keeping the discussion on track. | YES | NO | 3 |
| 15. Our team discusses issues openly and listens to all points of view before making decisions. | YES | NO | 3 |
| 16. Our team has a well-established repertoire of problem-solving, brainstorming, and decision-making techniques and uses them appropriately. | YES | NO | 3 |
| 17. The talents of each team member are recognized, affirmed, and utilized. | YES | NO | 3 |
| 18. Team members raise controversial issues in team meetings, rather than in "parking lot" meetings" (i.e., informal meetings held in small groups after the scheduled meeting). | YES | NO | 3 |
| 19. Our team has a repertoire of conflict resolution skills and uses them appropriately. | YES | NO | 3 |
| 20. Our team regularly plans for training to improve our decision-making skills. | YES | NO | 3 |
| 21. Team members identify and discuss multiple options before making a final decision and make every attempt not to "rush to judgment." | YES | NO | 3 |
| 22. Our team uses a variety of techniques for making decisions (e.g., voting, ranking, consensus) depending on the issue. | YES | NO | 3 |
| 23. Team members take turns assuming leadership roles, and no one individual dominates the team. | YES | NO | 3 |
| 24. Our team devotes time at each meeting for positive comments. | YES | NO | 3 |
| 25. Our team recognizes the importance of celebrating successes and sets aside time for doing so. | YES | NO | 3 |
| 26. Our team genuinely enjoys working together. | YES | NO | 3 |

Total possible points = 100

**OUR SCORE =** _____

> **RATE YOUR TEAM**
> Scoring Guide
>
> **0-25 points** Your team is in shambles, and if you accomplish anything, it's usually by accident and not by design. Get help soon.
>
> **26-50** Your team has some good things going for it but needs fine-tuning in many places. Set some realistic goals and spend as much time on process as you do on product. Get everybody on board.
>
> **51-75** Your team is well on its way to stardom, but unless you pay attention to the details, you could lose the support of all of the team members.
>
> **76-100** You're not there yet, but almost. Spend a meeting or two on goal setting that specifically relates to team process, and then pull together!

PROCESS NUMBER 6 — TEAM BUILDING

# TEAM BEHAVIOR CHECKLIST

### ■ DESCRIPTION

The Team Behavior Checklist is a set of eight indicators, each dealing with a specific aspect of team behavior. The descriptors are assigned point values from 1 to 5 based on a scale of descriptors. The total point value describes the overall effectiveness of the team's behavior.

### ■ APPLICATION

Use this instrument for a quick assessment of your team's effectiveness. The instrument would be helpful in the training of new members as well. The questions get at the personal feelings of team members in a way that some other scales do not.

### ■ TIME REQUIRED

Fifteen minutes to complete the scale and thirty minutes to process the results.

### ■ GROUP SIZE

Five to twenty team.

### ■ MATERIALS

One copy of the Team Behavior Checklist for each participant.

### ■ PROCESS

1. Distribute checklists to each group member and allow time for completion. Unless you expect group members to share their scores publicly, collect the completed checklists and process the information at another time.
2. Score and compute a team average for each of the eight items. Averages above 4.5 are exceptional and indicate a mature, effective team. Averages between 3.9 and 4.5 are excellent and indicate a team that is on its way.

Averages between 2.5 and 3.9 indicate that your team needs to spend time on team building activities in specific areas. Scores below 2.5 describe a team in trouble. Get help from a team-building consultant.

3. Discuss results of the questionnaire with the team and identify areas of needed growth.

---

### TEAM BEHAVIOR CHECKLIST

Instructions: Circle the number of the descriptor that best describes the behavior of your team.

INDICATOR 1: Team members are able to communicate openly with one another and say what they feel.

Scale of descriptors:

1. Discussion is inhibited and stilted. Team members hesitate to lay their true feelings on the table and are afraid of criticism, put-downs, and reprisals.
2. A few self-confident or politically connected team members speak openly, but most members are reluctant.
3. Many team members speak openly, but usually only after a communication trend has been established.
4. Although most communication is open, there are some topics which are taboo or select individuals who inhibit open communication with what they say or do.
5. Discussion is always free-wheeling and frank. There is no hesitation on the part of all team members to "tell it like it is" even in high-risk discussions and decision making. Team members feel free to express their feelings as well as their ideas.

INDICATOR 2: The individual abilities, knowledge, and experience of all team members are fully utilized.

Scale of descriptors:

1. The team is controlled by one individual who runs the show.
2. A select and chosen few do all the work.
3. At least half of the members do something, but the same people are always in charge.
4. A majority of the members participate, but no effort is made to share or exchange roles.
5. All team members are recognized as having gifts and talents that are fully utilized in accomplishing team goals, and roles are shared and exchanged. The chairperson (whoever is in that role) does not dominate.

INDICATOR 3: Conflict is resolved openly and effectively.

Scale of descriptors:

1. Team members suppress conflict and pretend it does not exist.
2. Team members recognize conflict but do not approach its solution directly and positively.
3. Team members recognize conflict and attempt to resolve it with some success, but they are sometimes clumsy and unskilled in their methodology, resulting in frequent misunderstandings.
4. Team members recognize conflict and can frequently resolve it through appropriate methods, but there are no standardized methodologies for handling conflict.
5. Team members are skilled at recognizing conflict and have a variety of conflict resolution strategies in their repertoire that they use with great success.

INDICATOR 4: Team members are committed to the vision and mission of the team.

Scale of descriptors:

1. Team members are openly committed to their own agendas and are unwilling to set aside personal goals for the team objective.
2. Team members pretend to be committed to the team objectives but frequently work at cross purposes.
3. A core of team members are committed, but a few naysayers and bystanders work to undermine the team's objectives when it serves their purposes.
4. The majority of team members are committed, but no intentional efforts have been made to work through any existing group differences.
5. Team members have worked through their differences, and they can honestly say they are committed to achieving the objectives of the team. Team processes are in place to assist members in accomplishing this goal.

INDICATOR 5: Team members can state their views openly without fear of ridicule or retaliation and let others do the same.

Scale of descriptors:

1. Team members never express views openly.
2. Team members sometimes express views openly, but it is usually done with hesitancy and reluctance.
3. Some team members feel free to express views openly, but many members are reluctant to express their true feelings.
4. Constructive criticism is accepted, but there are no mechanisms for ensuring that it is a regular aspect of teamwork.
5. Constructive criticism is frequent and frank; team members accept and encourage it. Group processes are used that intentionally monitor and encourage the free flow of opinions, ideas, and suggestions for improvement.

INDICATOR 6: Everyone accepts responsibility for keeping communication relevant and the team operation on track.

Scale of descriptors:

1. Meetings are usually disorganized and frequently off-task. Agendas are poorly constructed or exist only in the mind of a single individual.
2. One or two individuals consistently undermine the effectiveness of team meetings with "birdwalks," "sidebars," and inappropriate nonverbal language.
3. Meetings are run with an agenda and structure, but time limits are not monitored, and little of worth is accomplished.
4. Most team members accept accountability for the group's behavior, but the accomplishment of tasks is inconsistent.
5. Team members monitor one another's behavior, and all members take responsibility for the effectiveness of team meetings. Agenda items are routinely cared for and team business is accomplished effectively.

INDICATOR 7: Team members can get help from others on the team and give help without being concerned about hidden agendas.

Scale of descriptors:

1. Team members are reluctant to admit ignorance or the need for assistance. People are in the "independent" rather than "interdependent" mode.

2. Some team members will admit to the need for assistance, but many are territorial and competitive.

3. Team members want to be cooperative but lack the necessary skills.

4. Team members assist each other, but there is no systematic plan for evaluating the effectiveness of the cooperative atmosphere.

5. Team members have no reluctance in asking for help from others or in offering help to fellow members. There is transparency and trust between team members. Processes are used regularly to examine how well the team is working together and what may be interfering with its cooperation.

INDICATOR 8: The team climate is one of openness and respect for individual differences.

Scale of descriptors:

1. Team members are suspicious, competitive, and disrespectful.

2. A few team members are trying to improve the climate but are having a difficult time bringing about change.

3. The majority of team members work well together, but there are some who attempt to undermine a healthy climate.

4. The team works well together, but little is done to encourage, develop, and affirm this sense of teamwork.

5. Team members respect and affirm the unique gifts and talents of each member with appreciation for the variety of learning styles, personalities, and intelligences. The team takes time for team-building exercises that improve the climate.

**PROCESS NUMBER 7  TEAM BUILDING**

# CARD DISCOVERY PROBLEM

## ■ DESCRIPTION

This team building exercise is designed to highlight influence patterns, decision-making procedures, and the behavior of decision makers. A set of cards is distributed among the group. One card in the set is a singleton. The task of the group is to discover the singleton, following specific rules and within a specified time frame.

## ■ APPLICATION

This process can be helpful in demonstrating the importance of effective communication patterns, such as active listening and paraphrasing in group decision making.

## ■ TIME REQUIRED

Fifteen to thirty minutes for the problem solving and thirty minutes to debrief.

## ■ GROUP SIZE

One to five groups of five members each.

## ■ MATERIALS

Distribute four cards to each group member (twenty cards). In each set there will be a singleton. The other cards will have one or more duplicates.

## ■ PROCESS

1. Distribute a twenty-card set to each group (four cards per person).
2. Read the instructions aloud. You may wish to display them on the chalkboard or overhead as well.
   - A set of cards has been distributed to you. One card in the set is a singleton; it is unique. In other words, each card in the entire set has one or more duplicates, except the singleton card. Your task as a group is to discover the singleton card in the entire set. When your group indicates that the unique card has been identified, the task is ended whether or not you are correct, so be sure that everyone is confident of your choice before you declare.
   - You may organize yourselves any way you wish to complete the task with only the following restrictions:
     – You cannot show your cards to another member.
     – You may not pass cards to another member.
     – You must not look at another member's cards.
     – You cannot draw pictures or diagrams of the designs.
     – Do not refer to the numbers on the backs of the cards.
     – Do not pool your discards (i.e., keep your own discards in your own separate pile).
   - While it is very important that you do not make an error in selecting the unique card, you will be scored also for the amount of time it takes you to complete the task.
3. Instruct the participants to begin solving the problem.
4. After a decision has been reached, participants should discuss the influence and decision making that occurred during the exercise, compare their way of working on this problem with the way they usually work as a group, and attempt to identify the barriers that reduced effective use of group resources.

Adapted from *The Second Handbook of Organization Development in Schools*, Schmuck et al., Center for Educational Policy and Management, University of Oregon, 1977.

---

[1] R. S. Wellins, et al., *Empowered Teams*, (San Francisco: Jossey-Bass, 1991), 188.
[2] B. W. Tuckman. "Developmental Sequence in Small Groups," *Psychological Bulletin*, 1965, 63(6), 384–399.
[3] R. Lynch and T. Werner, *Continuous Improvement*, (Atlanta, Georgia: QualTeam, Inc., 1992), 121.
[4] Ibid., 122–125.
[5] Ibid., 125.
[6] Wellins, op cit., 189.
[7] G. M. Parker, *Team Players and Teamwork*, (San Francisco: Jossey-Bass, 1990), 65.
[8] Ibid., 61–98.
[9] Ibid., 100.
[10] Ibid., 57.

■ CHAPTER FOUR

# Group Processes for Generating Ideas

---
**WHAT IS CREATIVITY?**
---
**WHAT CAN INHIBIT CREATIVITY?**
---
**WHAT PROCESS ACTIVITIES CAN HELP MY TEAM GENERATE QUALITY IDEAS?**
---

## What is creativity?

If you've been a teacher, you will of course remember the very creative students that have passed through your classroom. They probably drove you to distraction with their divergent thinking, incessant questions about why you were doing things the way you were doing them, and their insatiable need to know.

> Discovery consists of looking at the same thing as everyone else and thinking something different.
> —Albert Szent-Gyorgyi

Creativity can often appear to be the last thing we're looking for as teams gather to solve problems and set goals. Team members with "off-the-wall" ideas are often put down by the more "practical" members of the team. Individuals with agendas and time lines frequently can't be bothered with processes like brainstorming; they want to "get the job done now."

> Ruth made a big mistake when he gave up pitching.
> —Tris Speaker, 1921

The problems we face, however, require creative and innovative solutions. As a team leader, you need to make time for generating creative ideas and giv-

65

> There is a curious notion that new ideas have to do with technical invention. This is a very minor aspect of the matter. New ideas are the stuff of change and progress in every field from science to art, from politics to personal happiness.
>
> —Edward de Bono

ing your team time to "chew on" a new solution to a problem.

Creativity has been defined in many ways, but my favorite description is this:

*An arbitrary harmony, an expected astonishment, a habitual revelation, a familiar surprise, a generous selfishness, an unexpected certainty, a formable stubbornness, a vital triviality, a disciplined freedom, an intoxicating steadiness, a repeated initiation, a difficult delight, a predictable gamble, an ephemeral solidity, a unifying difference, a demanding satisfier, a miraculous expectation, and an accustomed amazement.*[1]

## What can inhibit creativity?

If creativity is so important to the solution of difficult problems and meeting the challenges of the future, why do we immediately freeze up when someone suggests the application of creativity to a problem? "Oh, I'm not creative," will be the response of many. In addition to that typical response, here are nine other mental locks:

- The Right Answer
- That's Not Logical
- Follow the Rules
- Be Practical
- Avoid Ambiguity
- To Err Is Wrong
- Play Is Frivolous
- That's Not My Area
- Don't Be Foolish[2]

> I believe in intuition and inspiration . . . at times I feel certain that I am right while not knowing the reason . . . Imagination is more important than knowledge. For knowledge is limited, whereas imagination embraces the entire world, stimulating progress, giving birth to evolution. It is, strictly speaking, a real factor in scientific research.
>
> —Albert Einstein

Perhaps if you think of creativity as the generation of ideas or options, some of the pressure that is created when someone challenges us to be creative might be removed. Look upon creativity in the way that Edward de Bono describes it, as lateral thinking. "Lateral thinking is . . . concerned with breaking out of the concept prisons of old ideas. This leads to changes in attitude and approach; to looking in a different way at things which have always been looked at in the same old way."[3]

In his book, *Conceptual Blockbusting,* James Adams describes several conceptual blocks: "mental walls which block the problem-solver from correctly perceiving a problem or conceiving its solution."[4] Adams says we all have them: perceptual blocks (our senses just won't let us see the situation as it exists), cultural and environmental blocks (feelings, values, ethnic expectations), emotional blocks (embarrassment, lack of self-esteem), and intellectual and expressive blocks (our own inability to think and communicate as we would like). Knowing that these blocks exist can, in part, help us to be more sensitive to our own need to work on breaking through the barriers and to help members of our team become more creative problem solvers.

> Sensible and responsible women do not want to vote.
> —Grover Cleveland, 1905

> There is no likelihood man can ever tap the power of the atom.
> —Robert Millikan, Nobel Prize in Physics, 1920

## What process activities can help my team generate quality ideas?

The following process activities are designed to help your team generate a variety of ideas and options. They can help you overcome the blocks that were described earlier because they give people permission to act and think in ways that might be different. They encourage teams to ask questions and look at problems in new ways. Use these activities before you begin defining solutions and making action plans. Some of the activities are very simple and can be completed in a short time. Other processes are designed to take much longer and may require the assistance of a consultant or facilitator.

> Everything that can be invented has been invented.
> —Charles H. Duell, Director, U.S. Patent Office, 1899

Each process will contain six parts: 1. Description, 2. Application, 3. Time Required, 4. Group Size, 5. Materials, and 6. Process.

## PROCESS NUMBER 1 — GENERATING IDEAS

# BRAINSTORMING

### ■ DESCRIPTION

Brainstorming is a process in which a team generates as many ideas/solutions as rapidly as it can without regard for immediate quality. The process can be random, where individuals call out ideas as they occur to them, or more formal and structured, where individuals write out ideas and are called on in turn to respond.

### ■ APPLICATION

Brainstorming is a valuable technique when confronting a problem that may have many answers. It is also helpful when confronting a problem that has been "solved" in the past and keeps coming back to the team because the solutions aren't working.

### ■ TIME REQUIRED

Thirty minutes to one hour.

### ■ GROUP SIZE

Ideal group size is six to ten. Up to fifty or more participants are possible if the process is well-structured and facilitated.

### ■ MATERIALS

Chart paper and a variety of colored markers for the recorder.

### ■ PROCESS

1. Clearly define the question or problem for the group. Writing the question or problem on chart paper, chalkboard, or on an overhead will help visual learners to remain focused.
2. For **formal** or **structured brainstorming** ask participants to write (silently) within a specified time period (10–15 minutes) their own list of topics/ideas.

    In **random brainstorming,** participants need not write down their ideas. They share them in a rapid-fire verbal fashion. This version, however, can often short-circuit the individual who needs time to contemplate and might be intimidated by a "free-for-all" session where very verbal participants will dominate.

    In **reverse brainstorming**, participants generate all the reasons something might go wrong. This is a beneficial process to use after a solution has been selected (particularly if the solution is expensive and a mistake could have serious repercussions).

In small brainstorming groups (six or seven participants), the **trigger technique** is often used. A variation of the formal or structured brainstorming process, each participant completes a list and then reads it aloud to the group. After the reading of each list, there is a short brainstorming period, then another list is read, until all the lists have been read.

The following rules should be discussed before beginning the verbal brainstorming sessions:

- List every idea as it is given, no matter how far out it seems to be. One idea per person at a time.
- Quantity is the goal. Quality will follow.
- Don't prejudge whether your own ideas are good or bad, just call them out. Even silly ideas stimulate new, creative ideas in yourself and others.
- No intimidation of group members with body language or verbiage.
- Don't explain your idea—be brief. Don't ask others for help in phrasing.
- Don't try to sell your idea—simply state it.
- No discussion or comments until after the list is complete.
- Don't repeat an idea, but you can add to one already listed.
- Work quickly.
- Invite everyone to participate, but don't force it.
- When the flow of responses stops, the process will be ended.
- Squeeze out the last possible idea; it might generate a whole new line of thinking.

3. At the end of the time period, each person, in turn, presents his or her idea (no duplicates) to a recorder appointed by the chair.
4. After all ideas have been listed, allow time to review and/or clarify the topics.
5. The session can end at this time with another group or individual evaluating the ideas, or the participants can be asked to write on their own and in a specified time the ideas/solutions from the total list that they feel merit further attention and the reasons for their choices.
6. The participants then take turns presenting one of these positive choices (without duplicating) to a recorder who also lists the reasons for each choice. Time is provided for clarification.
7. The same process is then used for identifying, recording, and clarifying the ideas that each participant feels should not be studied and the reasons for these decisions.

8. Priorities are identified by having participants select and rank in priority order on their own five ideas from the list that they feel have the highest priority for study. The positive and negative reasons for studying each should also be given.

9. Brainstorming ideas must be evaluated and a process selected for determining which ideas will be considered in more depth or even used. Spending time on a brainstorming session without follow-up can be very bad for team morale.

Brainstorming process adapted from the following sources: Presentation by Dr. Wilma Smith on Site-Based Management, St. Charles, Illinois, 1989; *Discussing and Deciding* by Thomas M. Scheidel and Laura Crowell, New York: Macmillan Publishing Co., 1979; *Teaming for Quality Improvement* by H. David Shuster, Englewood Cliffs, New Jersey: Prentice Hall, 1990; *School-Based Improvement*, by Barbara J. Hansen and Carl L. Marburger, Columbia, Maryland: National Committee for Citizens in Education, 1989.

## PROCESS NUMBER 2 GENERATING IDEAS

# NOMINAL GROUP TECHNIQUE

### ■ DESCRIPTION

The Nominal Group Technique has been described as silent brainstorming, and the first part of the process is very similar to the formal brainstorming approach described in Process One, although more private in nature. Part Two of the process will assist teams in reducing the size of their list of items to those that should receive full evaluation.

### ■ APPLICATION

The Nominal Group Technique is a valuable process to use when confronting a problem that may have many answers. It is also helpful when teams are "stuck" on the same old solutions that don't seem to be working. This process also offers a quick and easy way to reduce the length of a list, giving every member an equal voice in the outcome. This approach will keep vocal team members from "running the show." If team members have been reluctant to share ideas in a public forum, the private nature of NGT will free them of inhibitions.

### ■ TIME REQUIRED

Sixty to ninety minutes.

### ■ GROUP SIZE

Five to thirty people.

### ■ MATERIALS

3 × 5 cards and pencils for participants. Chart paper and colored markers for the recorders. Masking tape or pushpins to mount the chart paper.

### ■ PROCESS

#### NOMINAL GROUP TECHNIQUE: PART ONE

1. Hang chart paper on walls prior to beginning of session. Provide enough chart paper to accommodate five or six ideas per sheet.

2. Clearly define the question or problem for the group. Writing the question or problem on chart paper, chalkboard, or on an overhead will help visual learners to remain focused.
3. Distribute two or three 3 × 5 cards to each participant (two cards if nine or more people, three cards if eight or fewer people).
4. Instruct participants to write one idea/solution/suggestion on each card. Use ten words or less. Print neatly. Allow five to ten minutes for this activity. (Another version of the NGT uses a round-robin recording of ideas similar to that used in formal brainstorming. Which method of "getting the ideas" you choose will depend on your group and its needs.)
5. Collect and shuffle cards for anonymity.
6. Ask for volunteers to write entries on chart paper, one person per sheet. Give all volunteers the same color marker (preferably dark); save the colored markers for part two.
   - No talking.
   - No more than six ideas per sheet, evenly spaced, with about six to eight inches between entries.
   - Do not number ideas.
   - Establish a six-inch left margin and draw a bullet on that margin at the beginning of each entry.
   - Absolutely no editing. Write each entry exactly as written on card, including spelling and/or syntax errors.
   - Be neat.
7. Ask volunteer recorders to return cards and markers to the facilitator.
8. Participants should read entries as they are being written on the sheets, search for surprising ideas, and try to think of additional items that are inspired by what they are reading. Write any newly inspired ideas on a sheet of paper for later entry.

## NOMINAL GROUP TECHNIQUE: PART TWO
### For Small Groups

1. Take each idea in turn and make certain that there is agreement and understanding about what each item means.
2. The team will now vote to reduce the initial list to a rank-ordered smaller list that they can discuss as a group. Each participant should rank order the five ideas/solutions that he or she feels are the most important. The most important idea receives a 5, the next a 4, and so on. Unranked items receive a zero.

3. Develop a chart to record the scores of each group member for his or her five most important ideas. Participants can give their rankings verbally to the chair, who will record them on the chart.

### For Larger Groups

1. In a larger group you may prefer to use the following method of ranking. Give each participant five 3 × 5 cards (seven if the list is very long). Ask participants to select the five most important items and write them out in the center of each card, one item per card. They should then write the item's designated number in the upper-left corner. While participants are doing this, prepare a tally sheet to record the votes by writing as many numbers as there are items under consideration in the voting. Give participants a four-minute time limit for choosing and writing their five items. When everyone has completed this task, give the following instructions:
   - Spread the cards out in front of you so that you can see all five at once. Decide which card is more important than all the others. Write 5 in the lower-right-hand corner and underline it three times. Turn the card over.
   - Which is the least important of the four remaining cards? Write 1 in the lower-right-hand corner and underline it three times. Turn the card over.
   - Select the most important of the three remaining cards. Write 4 in the lower-right-corner and underline it three times. Turn the card over.
   - Select the least important of the two cards that are left. Write 2 in the lower-right corner and underline it three times.
   - Write 3 in the lower-right-hand corner of the last card and underline it three times.
2. Collect the cards. They may be shuffled to communicate to the participants that their voting will be anonymous.
3. Ask someone to assist you in reading off the votes or in recording the numbers. The reason the rankings are underlined is to keep you from confusing them with the item numbers.

### For All Groups

1. Discuss the voting pattern.
2. Follow-up to the Nominal Group Technique will involve the interaction and discussion by group members regarding the highest ranked ideas/solutions and what action will be taken on the items.

<small>Materials for the Nominal Group Technique were adapted from *Discussing and Deciding: A Desk Book for Group Leaders and Members* by Thomas M. Scheidel and Laura Crowell, New York, Macmillan Publishing Co., 1979; *Teaming for Quality Improvement* by H. David Shuster, Englewood Cliffs, New Jersey: Prentice Hall, 1990; and *Group Techniques for Idea Building* by Carl M. Moore, Newbury Park, California: Sage Publications, 1987.</small>

**PROCESS NUMBER 3  GENERATING IDEAS**

# MIND MAPPING

### ■ DESCRIPTION

Mind Mapping is a process that can tap the creativity of those individuals who think visually rather than verbally. Participants write an issue, problem, or situation in a box in the center of a large piece of paper (rolled butcher paper works best) and then draw branches out from the center and label them with major headings. As ideas related to each category occur, limbs are drawn onto the branches and the ideas written there.

### ■ APPLICATION

When other forms of idea generation are getting a little stale, use this process to generate excitement and creativity.

### ■ TIME REQUIRED

Fifteen to thirty minutes.

### ■ GROUP SIZE

Five to twenty-five participants.

### ■ MATERIALS

Chart paper and colored markers.

### ■ PROCESS

Have each participant draw a mind map of a problem facing the team. After working alone, have the group combine all maps into one large one.

### ■ FOLLOW-UP

Mind maps are wonderful to hang up in a central location and add to as time goes by. A small group can begin a mind map and then ask the larger group to continue adding ideas/suggestions/solutions. I've known some groups who have left their mind maps displayed over an entire year.

This process was adapted from Continuous Improvement: Teams and Tools by Robert F. Lynch and Thomas J. Werner, Atlanta, Georgia: QualTeam, Inc., 1992.

# SAMPLE MIND MAP

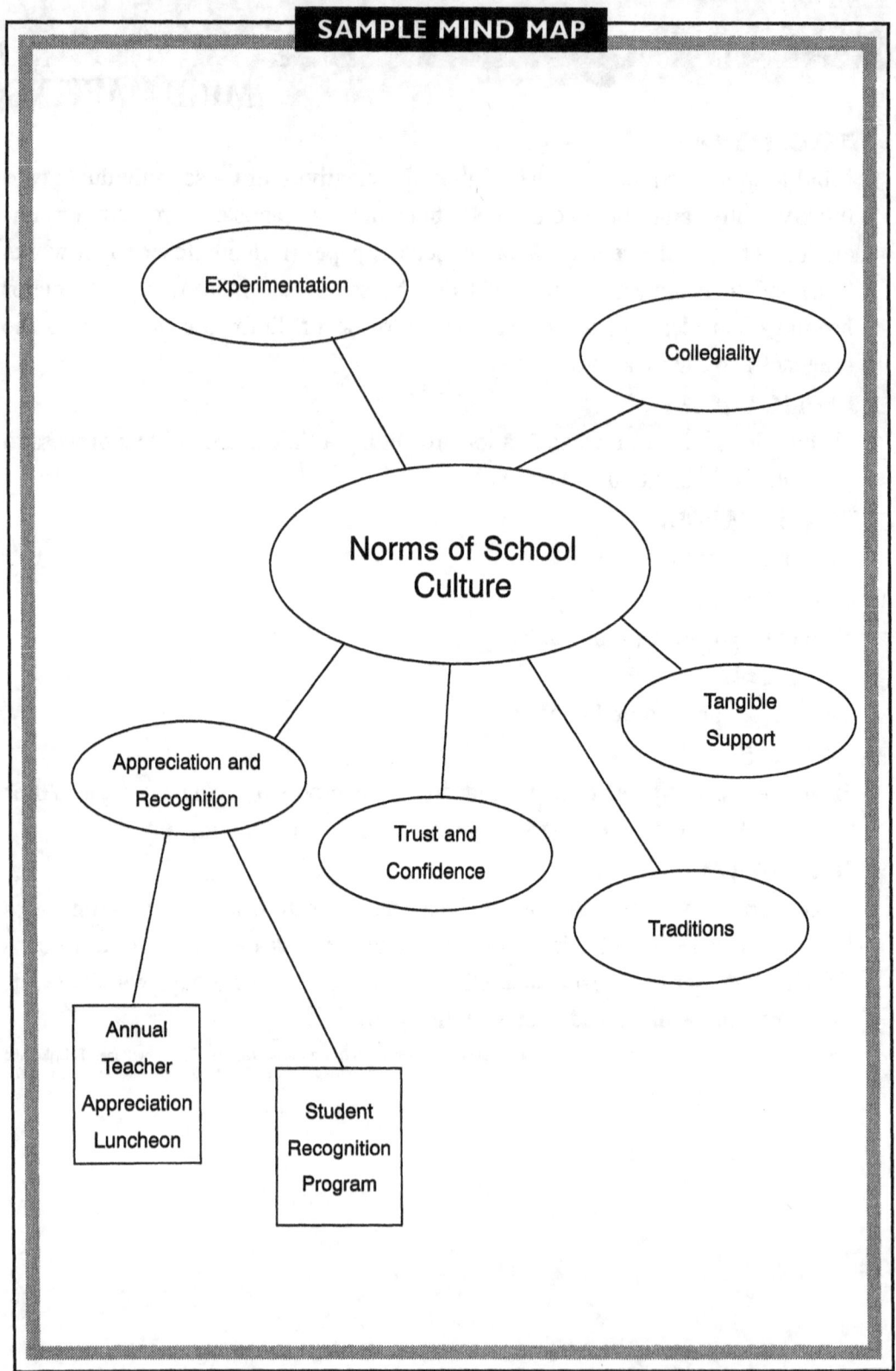

## Process Number 4 — Generating Ideas

# FAULT TREE ANALYSIS

### ■ DESCRIPTION

This process challenges team members to come up with problems rather than solutions through a kind of reverse-brainstorming process. The main problem is written on the trunk of a tree. Subproblems are written on the branches of the tree and the multiple problems that are offshoots of these become twigs on the tree. Participants list all of the possible reasons why something will not work or cannot occur.

### ■ APPLICATION

When you're "stuck" on a problem and there are multiple naysayers predicting doom and gloom, Fault Tree Analysis will illuminate even the tiniest of problems (right down to the twigs of the tree). When the problems are "out on the table," then your team's energies will be free to focus on solutions. This process can generate humor and often relieve the stress and anxiety that can be associated with overcoming the obstacles to solving a "big" problem.

### ■ TIME REQUIRED

Twenty to forty-five minutes.

### ■ GROUP SIZE

Five to fifteen participants.

### ■ MATERIALS

Chart paper, magic markers of different colors, masking tape.

### ■ PROCESS

1. Ask the most artistically talented member of the team to draw a large tree with a trunk and branches that are large enough to write words and phrases on.
2. Write the issue/problem/question under discussion on the trunk of the tree.
3. Ask participants to generate the subproblems of this issue and have the recorder write them on the branches of the tree.
4. Then ask participants to generate the "nit-pickiest" problems to write on the twigs of each branch.
5. Use a process of your choosing to generate solutions to solve the branch problems presented.

## PROCESS NUMBER 5 — GENERATING IDEAS

# CHECKLISTS

### ■ DESCRIPTION
The Checklists process is a detailed series of questions to expand the team's thinking about the range of possibilities for revising a procedure.

### ■ APPLICATION
This process is helpful when the team wants to change something (like a long-standing disciplinary process; the organizational structure for parent-teacher conferences; or the way the report card is designed).

### ■ TIME REQUIRED
Forty-five to ninety minutes.

### ■ GROUP SIZE
Five to fifteen participants.

### ■ MATERIALS
Chart paper and colored markers; pushpins or masking tape. A copy of the Osborn Checklist for each participant.

### ■ PROCESS
1. Clarify the problem for which the team will be trying to create a solution by changing a procedure or product.
2. Give each member a copy of the Osborn Checklist, which is a list of questions to be used to help participants open up their thinking.
3. Read one heading plus the subquestions. Record all suggestions on chart paper where all participants can see. No evaluative comments should be made at this point.
4. Read through all nine headings. Number each suggestion consecutively.
5. Some questions may generate no responses. That is acceptable. Move on.
6. Ask each participant to select three suggestions to be pursued by the group. Any suggestion that is named by more than two persons will remain in the shortened list, while the others remain in reserve.
7. Discuss each of the most favored suggestions in turn, listing advantages and disadvantages.
8. Poll once again to discover the three suggestions that are considered the best. Choose a second best.
9. Develop an action plan to implement the suggestions that were chosen.

The Checklists process was adapted from materials in *Applied Imagination* by Alex Osborn, New York: Charles Scribner & Sons, 1963; and *Discussing and Deciding* by Thomas M. Scheidel and Laura Crowell, New York: Macmillan Publishing Co., 1979.

## OSBORN CHECKLIST

Can It Be Put to Other Uses?
 New ways to use as is? Other uses if modified?

Can We Adapt It?
 What else is like this? What other ideas does this suggest? Does the past offer a parallel? What could we copy? Whom could we emulate?

How Can We Modify It?
 New twist? Change meaning, color, motion, sound, odor, form, shape? Other changes?

How Might We Magnify It?
 What to add? More time? Greater frequency? Stronger? Higher? Longer? Thicker? Extra value? Plus ingredient? Duplicate? Multiply? Exaggerate?

How Might We Minify It?
 What to subtract? Smaller? Condensed? Miniature? Lower? Shorter? Lighter? Omit? Streamline? Split up? Understate?

What Might We Substitute?
 Who else instead? What else instead? Other ingredient? Other material? Other process? Other power? Other place? Other approach? Other tone of voice?

What Could We Rearrange?
 Interchange components? Other pattern? Other layout? Other sequence? Transpose cause-and-effect? Change pace? Change schedule?

What Could Be Reversed?
 Transpose positive and negative? How about opposites? Turn it backward? Turn it upside down? Reverse roles? Change shoes? Turn tables?

How Could We Combine?
 How about a blend, an alloy, an assortment, an ensemble? Combine unit? Combine purposes? Combine appeals? Combine ideas?

SOURCE: From Osborn, Alex F., *Applied Imagination.* Copyright © 1963. Reprinted with permission from the copyright holder, The Creative Education Foundation, 1050 Union Road, Buffalo, NY 14224.

## PROCESS NUMBER 6 — GENERATING IDEAS

# IDEAWRITING

### ■ DESCRIPTION

Ideawriting is a process that permits a large group of individuals to think about a question or problem, react to it in writing, react in turn to what other members of a small group have written about the issue, and then together summarize their discussion. Ideawriting is also called brainwriting by some authors.

### ■ APPLICATION

This process is ideal for accomplishing a great deal with a large group of people in a relatively short period of time. All members of the group must be willing to write, but everyone will be able to have equal participation. All groups can respond to the same question; groups can be assigned different questions; or groups can choose the question to which they will respond.

### ■ TIME REQUIRED

Fifteen to twenty minutes for silent writing. Fifteen to twenty minutes for written reaction/interaction.

### ■ GROUP SIZE

Small groups must be from three to six persons maximum. The ideal size is three or four. Groups as large as 700 people have used this process to generate ideas on a topic at a large conference.

### ■ MATERIALS

Notepads and pencils for each individual. Chart paper and markers for summarizing group findings.

### ■ PROCESS

1. Divide the large group into small groups of three to six individuals.
2. Ask the group to choose someone to serve as the group leader. The group leader will be responsible for keeping the group on task.
3. Write the question/problem/stimulus in a location where all participants can easily refer to it during the process.
4. Each participant should write his or her name in the upper-right-hand corner of his or her notepad, write the question/problem/stimulus at the top of the pad, and write a response to the question.
5. When participants have completed their responses, they should place their pads in the center of the table. Each participant should then select a pad other than his or her own, read what is written, and then write a brief response.

Participants can offer solutions, qualify what is written, add suggestions, or point out weaknesses. This process should be repeated until every participant has responded to each of the other participants at the table.

6. In some cases, the process could now be considered complete, and a small team would evaluate the results of the process. In other cases, the group can discuss, analyze, and report its findings.
7. If this is the case, the group will summarize its findings on a sheet of chart paper and choose a reporter to share the findings with the large group.
8. Each group will report back to the large group.
9. A small writing group, task force, or leadership team will examine the findings and take the next step.

This process was adapted from materials in *Group Techniques for Idea Building* by Carl M. Moore, Newbury Park, California: Sage Publications, 1987; and *Consensus Methodologies* by J. N. Warfield, Charlottesville, Virginia: Center for Interactive Management, 1982.

## PROCESS NUMBER 7 GENERATING IDEAS

# THE KIVA TECHNIQUE

### ■ DESCRIPTION

This name of this process is taken from the kiva process used by the Hopi Indians to make important tribal decisions. The kiva was the structure in which the deliberations took place. In the kiva process, the key decision-making body (the tribal elders in the Hopi tribe) conducted an open discussion leading to a preliminary decision. Circles of other groups sat around this body and listened to the discussion, but did not participate. After the key decision-making body's discussion was complete, the next circle of individuals moved to the center to discuss what they thought they heard and how they felt about it. Each succeeding group moved to the center until the key decision-making body was back in the center again.

### ■ APPLICATION

This process could be used in an organizational setting where a key decision-making body wants everyone in the organization to be a part of the discussion. Group members do not necessarily have an opportunity to participate in the preliminary decision, but the leadership group will have the benefit of hearing reactions and reactions to reactions from a variety of perspectives before making the final decision.

### ■ TIME REQUIRED
Ninety minutes to two hours.

### ■ GROUP SIZE
Twenty-five to fifty participants.

### ■ MATERIALS
None

### ■ PROCESS
1. Arrange the room so that concentric circles of chairs can be arranged to accommodate each group of individuals that will participate in the kiva process.
2. The discussion of the key body should be allowed to get all of the key issues out on the table, but care should be taken not to "ramble" or become repetitive.
3. The reaction groups should be given twenty to thirty minutes.

### ■ FOLLOW-UP
The key decision-making group must convene to discuss what was heard from the various groups and determine if any changes must be made to the original decision in order to accommodate the needs of the groups.

This process was adapted from materials in Making Tough Decisions: Tactics for Improving Managerial Decision Making by Paul C. Nutt, San Francisco: Jossey-Bass, 1989.

---

[1] G. M. Prince, *The Practice of Creativity*, (New York: Harper & Row, Publishers, 1970), xiii.
[2] von Oech, *A Whack on the Side of the Head*, (New York: Warner Books, 1983), 9.
[3] E. de Bono, *Lateral Thinking: Creativity Step by Step*, (New York: Harper & Row, Publishers, 1970), 11.
[4] J. Adams, *Conceptual Blockbusting*, (Stanford, California: Stanford Alumni Association, 1974), 11.

■ CHAPTER FIVE

# Group Processes for Sharing Critical Information

---
**HOW CAN I MAKE SURE MY INFORMATION IS ACCURATE AND SUFFICIENT?**
---
**HOW DO I KNOW WHEN THE TEAM HAS ENOUGH INFORMATION TO MAKE A DECISION?**
---
**WHAT ARE SOME WAYS TO SHARE RESEARCH AND INFORMATION WITH MY TEAM?**
---

## How can I make sure my information is accurate and sufficient?

We are constantly confronted with statistics about the information explosion, and, although a relatively recent concept, the "information superhighway" is already experiencing traffic jams. Information is a critical aspect of quality decision making. It must be accurate and there must be enough of it.

> People cannot keep all the pros and cons in mind at one time.
> —Benjamin Franklin

"Information is substantive knowledge conveying meaningful insights about some topic of interest. Data are specific isolated bits of measurement (usually numerical) that verify the degree of truth or falsity of information."[1] Information and data can come in the form of historical case studies, graphs and charts, research studies, experiences of individuals, the opinions and judgment of experts in the field, trend studies, summary reports, surveys and needs assessments, test data, or market research. Making decisions without information is foolish, if not suicidal.

> **H**ow can the manager [leader] improve his performance in analyzing problems? The key to the answer lies in the fundamental fact that the raw material of management is information.
>
> —Charles H. Kepner and Benjamin B. Tregoe

Making sure you have enough of the right kind of information and that this information is adequately shared with all team members who will be making the decision is first and foremost the responsibility of the leader. Behaviors such as withholding key information or relying on a source with a vested interest is self-serving and morally reprehensible.

There are several questions that can be asked to determine if information meets the criteria of accuracy and sufficiency:

- Is the information as presented accurate, correct, and true?
- Is the information appropriate? Does it fit exactly what the group is discussing? Are the cases presented typical and representative, or are they atypical and unusual examples?
- Is the information the most recent available? Or is it dated? Is it collected at an appropriate time for the specific question being considered?
- Are all of the pieces of information consistent with each other? Do they fit together in a meaningful pattern?
- Are the sources accurately quoted? Is there any chance the statements could have been taken out of context?
- Is the source truly an expert on this matter? An expert in one field may not be an expert in another.
- Is the source reliable? Is the source known to be dependable for providing sound evidence?
- Is the source known to have any special bias or prejudice on the topic?
- Will the source profit personally if his or her testimony is accepted? The most convincing expert is one who testifies counter to his or her own special interests.[2]

## How do I know when the team has enough information to make a decision?

Gathering information, while an important step in making decisions, can often become an end in itself for many teams. As long as they are researching the issue, they can defer the decision to another day.

I share this humorous checklist, which has guided my work with teams in the past. You know you've done enough research when:

- you've exceeded the budget line item for paper and the fiscal year is only half over;
- your secretary refuses to call any more schools or districts to find out what they're doing;
- consultants/experts rarely return your telephone calls;
- team members stop coming to meetings because they've begun to believe that nothing will ever happen; and
- your boss keeps asking for a date by which he or she can expect a decision.

> Throughout the thinking process group members must ask whether they have accurate facts and sufficient facts: accurate in what they tell us and sufficient in covering all aspects that need to be covered.
>
> —Thomas M. Scheidel and Laura Crowell

## What are some ways to share research and information with my team?

Burning up the photocopy machine is one way to share information with your team. And the best team leaders do pass along articles and newsclippings to their team members regularly. Networking with individuals who have special expertise is another. Attending conferences and meetings where many options are presented for consideration is still another. There are also a variety of structured processes that can help you organize to present critical information to your team. Some are best used with small teams and others are suitable for large organizational groups.

Each process will contain six parts: 1. Description, 2. Application, 3. Time Required, 4. Group Size, 5. Materials, and 6. Process.

## PROCESS NUMBER 1 — SHARING CRITICAL INFORMATION

# COOPERATIVE GROUPS

### ■ DESCRIPTION

Participants work together and process new material as a group. The interaction and other aspects of cooperative learning ensure that the material will be discussed, considered, and digested more thoroughly than if the information had merely been assigned to be read silently.

### ■ APPLICATION

Cooperative Groups work particularly well when research, new ideas, new content, or new teaching approaches must be shared with a large group such as a faculty. Cooperative Groups ensure that critical questions will be raised in a forum where answers can quickly be provided.

### ■ TIME REQUIRED

One to two hours depending on the complexity of the material.

### ■ GROUP SIZE

Ten to thirty participants.

### ■ MATERIALS

A copy of the teaching materials for each participant.

### ■ PROCESS

1. Divide the large group into cooperative learning groups that can range in size from two to six. Individuals may be assigned to a group at random or on the basis of special interest or level (e.g., all of the fourth-grade teachers; all of the special-area teachers). The groups may last for as short a period as two or three minutes or as long as several weeks. Use any of the following methods:
   - Use cooperative learning to keep participants actively engaged in a lecture:
     - Pre-Focused Discussion: Prior to the lecture, prepare questions on an overhead transparency or chart paper. Have participants discuss the questions in pairs. The discussion is aimed at promoting advance organizing for the lecture ahead.
     - Turn-to-Your-Partner Discussions: Divide the lecture into ten- to fifteen-minute segments. This is about the length of time an adult can concentrate on a lecture. Plan a short discussion task to be given to pairs of audience members. You may:

- Summarize the answer to the question being discussed.
- Give a reaction to the theory, concepts, or information being presented.
- Elaborate (relate material to past learning so that it gets integrated into existing conceptual frameworks) the material being presented.
- Predict what is going to be presented next.
- Attempt to resolve the conceptual conflict the presentation has aroused.
- Hypothesize answers to the questions being posed.
  - Make sure that participants are randomly called upon to share their answers after each discussion task. Such individual accountability ensures that the groups take the tasks seriously.
  - Post-Focused Discussion: Prepare a discussion task to summarize what participants have learned from the lecture.

2. Use cooperative learning to make participants responsible for all learning activities. Distribute instructional materials among group members so that all group members will participate and learn. Materials can be disseminated in a number of different ways:
   - Give one copy of the materials to the group so that the members will have to work together.
   - Give a set of materials to a group so that each member has only one part of the total. Individual group members can then become experts on their part and "teach" it to the rest of the group.

Adapted from David W. Johnson and Roger T. Johnson, *Leading the Cooperative School*,<br>Edina, Minnesota: Interaction Book Company, 1989.

---

**PROCESS NUMBER**  **SHARING CRITICAL INFORMATION**

# THE GALLERY

## ■ DESCRIPTION

In The Gallery process, participants move from station to station where they share their knowledge on a particular topic or question. As the group "pools" its knowledge, a full picture will emerge that is more complete than that "painted" by any one individual.

## ■ APPLICATION

When specialized knowledge/information on a broad range of subjects is required from the group, setting up a gallery to "paint a picture" of the desired subject is helpful. The small groups encourage discussion and many ideas are generated as participants see what others have written.

### ■ TIME REQUIRED
Forty-five to ninety minutes.

### ■ GROUP SIZE
Ten to forty participants.

### ■ MATERIALS
Chart paper and colored markers; pushpins or masking tape.

### ■ PROCESS
1. Divide group into pairs or triads. Each subgroup should contain enough different perspectives to encourage discussion in the larger group.
2. Post pieces of chart paper around the room. These will represent "the gallery." Each chart paper will represent different categories of the subject under discussion.
3. Give each group a different colored marker.
4. At two- to three-minute intervals, each group rotates to a new "portrait" and adds its contributions to the list. No items can be repeated. If a group has nothing new to add, it writes nothing.
5. At the end of the gallery exercise, the materials should be collated and provided to the group for further refinement and discussion at a later time.

Adapted from the Home and School Institute Workshop MegaSkills Training. Washington, D.C.

---

## PROCESS NUMBER 3 — SHARING CRITICAL INFORMATION

# THE SYMPOSIUM

### ■ DESCRIPTION
A Symposium is a group of talks, lectures, or speeches presented by several individuals on various phases of a single subject or problem.

### ■ APPLICATION
Use this process when a large number of people need exposure to many facets of a single subject or problem. The approach is excellent for presenting basic information, facts, or points of view.

### ■ TIME REQUIRED
Half day to full day.

### GROUP SIZE
Fifty to three hundred people.

### MATERIALS
Presenters will provide their own printed materials. Overheads, chart paper, chalkboards, and other audiovisual equipment as needed.

### PROCESS
1. Identify the objective of the symposium.
2. Identify outside resource speakers and in-house experts to participate.
3. Meet with the speakers to set forth the specific objectives.
4. Invite participants and notify them of the symposium's objectives.
5. Communicate to participants how you wish them to use the information they have gained from the symposium.
6. Plan further events where small groups will react to the information, problem-solve, or develop action plans.

Material adapted from *Leadership and Dynamic Group Action* by George M. Beal, Joe M. Bohlen, and J. Neil Raudabaugh. Ames, Iowa: The Iowa State University Press, 1962.

PROCESS NUMBER 4 — SHARING CRITICAL INFORMATION

# THE PANEL DISCUSSION

### DESCRIPTION
The Panel Discussion is a discussion before an audience by a selected group of individuals (usually three to six) under the leadership of a moderator. The discussion is informal and conversational and permits the audience to "eavesdrop" on experts talking about their special fields of interest.

### APPLICATION
When the group needs to hear a variety of points of view so they can begin to form their own opinions, this process works well. This process is more informal than the symposium and is often useful for a controversial topic that no one wants to tackle head-on. The panel spreads responsibility.

### TIME REQUIRED
One hour to ninety minutes.

### GROUP SIZE
Fifty to one hundred in the large group. Three to seven (plus moderator) on the panel.

## MATERIALS

Advance reading materials may be given to participants. A transcript of the panel discussion may be provided to participants at a later time.

## PROCESS

1. Identify the objectives of the panel discussion.
2. Select panel members with care. Individuals should be chosen who are acknowledged experts in their field, articulate, and willing to express themselves before a group and interact with other panel members. Avoid panel members who can't "share the limelight." They will often "hog" the microphone and make it difficult for the moderator to gain control.
3. Meet with panel members beforehand to agree upon the scope of the discussion. Panel members might submit possible questions for consideration to the moderator.
4. Seat quiet panel members in the middle and lively panel members at either end.
5. Introduce the panel members to the group. Explain the ground rules and time limits.
6. Open the discussion with a question that will immediately focus on a critical attribute of the problem.
7. Present a final summary.
8. Turn the microphone back to the chairperson.
9. Communicate to participants your expectations for how they will use the information they have acquired: think about it, discuss it with colleagues, experiment with it in practice, or be prepared to give an opinion about it when asked at a later date.

Material adapted from *Leadership and Dynamic Group Action* by George M. Beal, Joe M. Bohlen, and J. Neil Raudabaugh. Ames, Iowa: The Iowa State University Press, 1962, pp. 206-213.

---

PROCESS NUMBER  SHARING CRITICAL INFORMATION

# THE INTERROGATOR PANEL

## DESCRIPTION

The Interrogator Panel is a slight variation on the traditional panel discussion in which a small group of knowledgeable individuals (the panel) and another small group of individuals (the interrogators) interact with one another with leadership from a moderator.

## APPLICATION

This process can be used when many facets of a complex problem need to be explored, when interest needs to be stimulated in a current problem, or when several experts are available and questioning them in a panel format would be beneficial.

## TIME REQUIRED

One to two hours.

## GROUP SIZE

Twenty-five to one hundred.

## MATERIALS

Advance reading materials may be given to participants. A transcript of the panel discussion may be provided to participants at a later time.

## PROCESS

1. Identify the objectives of the panel discussion.
2. Select panel members and interrogators with care. Individuals should be chosen who are acknowledged experts in their fields, articulate, and willing to express themselves before a group and interact with others. Avoid panel members or interrogators who can't "share the limelight." They will often "hog" the microphone and make it difficult for the moderator to gain control.
3. Meet with all participants beforehand to agree upon the scope of the discussion. Both panel members and interrogators might submit possible questions for consideration to the moderator. Audience members might be asked to submit questions for the interrogators to ask as well.
4. Seat panel members and interrogators so that all participants can see each other. A wide "V" shaped arrangement will work well. Seat lively members at either end and quiet ones in the middle.
5. Introduce the panel members and interrogators to the group. Explain the ground rules and time limits.
6. Open the discussion with a question that will immediately focus on a critical attribute of the problem.
7. Present a final summary.
8. Turn the microphone back to the chairperson.
9. Communicate to participants your expectations for how they will use the information they have acquired: think about it, discuss it with colleagues, experiment with it in practice, or be prepared to give an opinion about it when asked at a later date.

*Material adapted from* Leadership and Dynamic Group Action *by George M. Beal, Joe M. Bohlen, and J. Neil Raudabaugh. Ames, Iowa: The Iowa State University Press, 1962, pp. 214-221.*

**PROCESS NUMBER 6  SHARING CRITICAL INFORMATION**

# THE COMMITTEE HEARING

## ■ DESCRIPTION

The Committee Hearing is a method traditionally used by the United States Congress, but the questioning of one individual by several persons can be used in an informal setting as well.

## ■ APPLICATION

Use this process when a consultant or expert needs to be interviewed by the group. A small panel can interview the expert with the larger group as audience, or the team can interview the expert in an informal setting. This process is especially helpful if the expert is a poor speaker who tends to be disorganized and verbose, is evasive, or is so clever with words and argumentation techniques that it would be difficult for any one person to handle him or her.

## ■ TIME REQUIRED

One hour to ninety minutes.

## ■ GROUP SIZE

Interviewing committee of five or six members. Audience could be as large as fifty to one hundred.

## ■ MATERIALS

Advance reading may be required for committee members to be adequately prepared for the hearing.

## ■ PROCESS

1. Determine the objectives of the hearing.
2. Identify the expert who will testify at the hearing.
3. Identify a questioning committee.
4. Meet with the questioning committee to think through all aspects of the problem, the framework for questioning, procedures, and time limits.
5. Assign responsibilities for introductions. Make clear to the group what the qualifications of the expert are.
6. Carry out the interview.
7. Give a final summary.
8. Communicate to participants your expectations for how they will use the information they have acquired: think about it, discuss it with colleagues, experiment with it in practice, or be prepared to give an opinion about it when asked at a later date.

Material adapted from *Leadership and Dynamic Group Action* by George M. Beal, Joe M. Bohlen, and J. Neil Raudabaugh. Ames, Iowa: The Iowa State University Press, 1962, pp. 222-229.

**PROCESS NUMBER 7 SHARING CRITICAL INFORMATION**

# THE DIALOGUE

### ■ DESCRIPTION
The Dialogue is a discussion centered on a specific topic that is carried on in front of a group by two knowledgeable people.

### ■ APPLICATION
This process would be used to present facts, opinions, or points of view regarding a specific issue or problem.

### ■ TIME REQUIRED
One hour to ninety minutes.

### ■ GROUP SIZE
Twenty to one hundred participants.

### ■ MATERIALS
Participants may be asked to read materials in advance of the dialogue.

### ■ PROCESS
1. Select the topic to be discussed.
2. Identify two knowledgeable individuals to carry on the dialogue. They could be team members who will share critical information with the group or outside experts, but in either case they will need to work together, guide the conversation, and without embarrassment or self-consciousness interact in an informal and relaxed way.
3. Meet with the dialogue members to establish the framework, develop a tentative outline, determine timelines for major topics, and identify responsibilities for summarizing and providing transitions. The dialogue should not be scripted or read, but rather should be informal and spontaneous. Avoid "rehearsing" a dialogue. It will be deadly.
4. Introduce the topic and the dialogue members. Create an atmosphere of "eavesdropping."
5. Summarize the main points.
6. Communicate to participants your expectations for how they will use the information they have acquired: think about it, discuss it with colleagues, experiment with it in practice, or be prepared to give an opinion about it when asked at a later date.

Material adapted from *Leadership and Dynamic Group Action* by George M. Beal, Joe M. Bohlen, and J. Neil Raudabaugh. Ames, Iowa: The Iowa State University Press, 1962, pp. 230-234.

## PROCESS NUMBER 8 — SHARING CRITICAL INFORMATION

# THE INTERVIEW

### ■ DESCRIPTION
The Interview is the questioning of an expert on a given subject by an interviewer who usually represents the group.

### ■ APPLICATION
This process is less formal than a lecture or speech, but more formal than a dialogue. When the expert may be ill at ease or evasive on a topic, the interviewer can bridge the gap and create a psychological bridge between the expert and the group. When the expert may have several prepared presentations that do not meet the needs of the group but also has substantial knowledge that could benefit the group, the interview can serve both the group and the expert.

### ■ TIME REQUIRED
One hour.

### ■ GROUP SIZE
Twenty-five to fifty.

### ■ MATERIALS
Advance reading materials may be given to the group.

### ■ PROCESS
1. Identify the objective of the interview.
2. Identify the expert.
3. Identify the interviewer.
4. The interviewer and expert should meet to establish rapport, determine the major areas of questioning, the procedure to be followed, and the timelines.
5. Introduce the interviewer and the expert.
6. Summarize and close.
7. Communicate to participants your expectations for how they will use the information they have acquired: think about it, discuss it with colleagues, experiment with it in practice, or be prepared to give an opinion about it when asked at a later date.

Material adapted from *Leadership and Dynamic Group Action* by George M. Beal, Joe M. Bohlen, and J. Neil Raudabaugh. Ames, Iowa: The Iowa State University Press, 1962, pp. 235-239.

## PROCESS NUMBER 9 — SHARING CRITICAL INFORMATION

# THE LECTURE

### ■ DESCRIPTION

The Lecture is the most common process for delivering information from one individual to a group. It is often boring unless the lecturer is a gifted and entertaining public speaker.

### ■ APPLICATION

This process is useful to present information in a formal and direct manner; to supply expert information with continuity; to inspire and motivate a group; and to help a group share the experiences of another person vicariously. A group has to "want to learn" to respond well to the average lecture. The Lecture is not useful in the following settings:

- Bringing out divergent points of view on a subject (use a symposium).
- Moving a group toward consensus (use huddle or buzz groups for that).
- Bringing about a resolution of differences of opinion in a group (use a panel discussion for that).
- Bringing the most interesting and unique experiences of a person to the group (use the interview for that).
- Showing the group another point of view in a controversial situation (use role playing for that).

### ■ TIME REQUIRED

Forty minutes to one hour.

### ■ GROUP SIZE

Twenty to one hundred.

### ■ MATERIALS

Advance reading materials may be helpful to group members.

### ■ PROCESS

1. Identify the information needed and the purpose of the lecture.
2. Choose a qualified speaker.
3. Inform the speaker how his or her presentation will fit into the overall plan of the group.
4. Introduce the speaker and establish the framework.

5. Thank the speaker.
6. Communicate to participants your expectations for how they will use the information they have acquired: think about it, discuss it with colleagues, experiment with it in practice, or be prepared to give an opinion about it when asked at a later date.

Material adapted from *Leadership and Dynamic Group Action* by George M. Beal, Joe M. Bohlen, and J. Neil Raudabaugh. Ames, Iowa: The Iowa State University Press, 1962, pp. 240-245.

---

[1]H. D. Schuster, *Teaming for Quality Improvement,* (Englewood Cliffs, New Jersey: Prentice Hall, 1990), 103.

[2]T. M. Scheidel and L. Crowell, *Discussing and Deciding,* (New York: Macmillan Publishing Co., Inc., 1979), 18.

# CHAPTER SIX

# Group Processes for Problem Solving

---
**WHAT KINDS OF PROBLEMS ARE OUT THERE?**
---
**WHAT ARE THE CHARACTERISTICS OF GOOD PROBLEM SOLVERS?**
---
**WHAT ARE THE SEVEN STEPS TO PROBLEM SOLVING?**
---
**WHAT PROCESS ACTIVITIES CAN PROMOTE PRODUCTIVE PROBLEM SOLVING?**
---

I love problems. I love trying to solving them. I even get bored when there aren't enough of them, so I write a twice-monthly question/answer column for parents, helping them solve their problems. Of course, solving problems on the pages of a newspaper in two hundred words is nothing like solving problems with real-live people.

If you don't love problems enough to go out looking for them, then you're probably miserable in a leadership role. If your colleagues and teammates ever get the feeling that you don't want to hear bad news, you won't. Everyone but you will know the sky is falling. And there are many ways you can avoid facing problems:

> The mere formulation of a problem is often far more essential than its solution.
> —*Albert Einstein*

- Make it clear to colleagues that anyone who brings you a problem is rocking the boat;
- Get bogged down in administrivia so you will be too busy to handle any problems (which will leave your secretary and others to pick up the pieces); and

- Keep your schedule so tightly structured that it will protect you from the real world, which is teeming with problems of every kind.

## What kinds of problems are out there?

Problems can be classified and organized in a variety of ways: by the approaches we use to solve them; how the problem is structured; where in the organization the problem occurs; and whether the problem is a crisis situation or an opportunity to bring about change in a positive way.

### APPROACHES WE USE

The problems we face on a daily basis fall into one of three categories: analytical, creative, or judgmental. Analytical problems are ones that can be solved with mathematics and logic. There is a single right answer and the question is simply which formula will help us get it. We don't get many of those problems in education. Instead, we're usually faced with the creative and judgmental problems, the problems with fuzzy answers and multiple solutions. These solutions aren't the "black and white," "yes or no" kinds that present themselves to analytical problems.

> There is always an easy solution to every human problem—neat, plausible, and wrong.
> 
> —H. L. Mencken

Creative problems drive analytical minds to distraction. They have an infinite number of solutions, some practical and some downright crazy. Many inventions were the result of creative problem solving.

Judgmental problems need decisions that often deal with moral issues of right and wrong, or issues of "should we or shouldn't we?" Should we change the way we evaluate students? Should we implement multi-age groupings? Should we create an interdisciplinary studies department? As with creative problems, the solutions to judgmental problems are never definitive or easy.

### THE STRUCTURE OF PROBLEMS

Problems can have predictable, patterned structures (problems that occur fairly routinely and have standardized procedures for solutions) or they can be messy ones that need judgment, intuition, creativity, and superhuman problem-solving skills.

### WHERE PROBLEMS OCCUR

Another way of examining problems is to determine where in the organization they are occurring. Operational problems are those encountered on a day-to-day basis. While these are important problems to solve, they do not offer the challenge and excitement of the strategic-level problems that occur when engaging in problem solving that can impact the education of thousands of children.

CRISIS OR OPPORTUNITY

A final way of categorizing problems is to decide whether they are crises that needs to be dealt with immediately or opportunities that give decision makers the chance to be proactive rather than reactive.

Regardless of where your problem falls on the continuum or in which category you wish to place it, good problem-solving skills are essential.

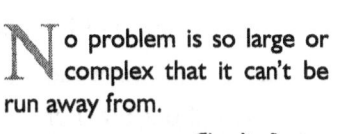

No problem is so large or complex that it can't be run away from.
—Charlie Brown

## What are the characteristics of good problem solvers?

The characteristics of good problem solvers are amazingly similar to the qualities one needs to be a good parent or a good marriage partner: patience, discipline, creativity, continuous improvement, repetition, honesty, and continuous learning.[1] Problem solving that is always a part of quality decision making does not come without struggle, frustration, and occasional bouts of chaos and messiness.

## What are the seven steps to problem solving?

Every theorist has developed his or her own model of problem solving, but most include these seven steps as "must-dos":

1. Define the problem.
2. Identify the suspected causes.
3. Verify the most likely causes.
4. Identify possible solutions.
5. Determine the best solutions.
6. Develop an action plan to implement the best solutions.
7. Evaluate action plans.[2]

## What process activities can promote productive problem solving?

The following process activities are designed to help your team become more effective and productive problem solvers. They will give structure and organization to what can often be a fragmented and frustrating journey. The processes that follow will assist at various points in the problem-solving process. Some will help with defining the problem, some will show ways to identify possible solutions, and still others will assist in selecting the best solution for your problem.

Each process will contain six steps: 1. Description, 2. Application, 3. Time Required, 4. Group Size, 5. Materials, and 6. Process.

## PROCESS NUMBER 1 — PROBLEM SOLVING

# NOMINAL GROUP TECHNIQUE

### ■ DESCRIPTION

The Nominal Group Technique has been described as silent brainstorming and was also included in Chapter Four as a process for generating ideas. While Part One of the process is very similar to the formal brainstorming approach described earlier, Part Two of the process will assist teams in reducing the size of their list to a smaller list of items that will receive full evaluation.

### ■ APPLICATION

The Nominal Group Technique is a valuable process to use when confronting a problem that may have many answers. It is also helpful when teams are "stuck" on the same old solutions that don't seem to be working. This process also offers a quick and easy way to reduce the length of a list, giving every member an equal voice in the outcome. This approach will keep vocal team members from "running the show." If team members have been reluctant to share ideas in a public forum, the private nature of NGT will free them of inhibitions.

### ■ TIME REQUIRED

Sixty to ninety minutes.

### ■ GROUP SIZE

Five to thirty participants.

### ■ MATERIALS

3 × 5 cards and pencils for participants. Chart paper and colored markers for the recorders. Masking tape or pushpins to mount the chart paper.

### ■ PROCESS

#### NOMINAL GROUP TECHNIQUE: PART ONE

1. Hang chart paper on walls prior to beginning of session. Provide enough chart paper to accommodate five or six ideas per sheet.
2. Clearly define the question or problem for the group. Writing the question or problem on chart paper, chalkboard, or overhead will help visual learners to remain focused.
3. Distribute two or three 3 × 5 cards to each participant (two cards if nine or more people, three cards if eight or fewer people).
4. Instruct participants to write one idea/solution/suggestion on each card. Use ten words or less. Print neatly. Allow five to ten minutes for this activity.

(Another version of the NGT uses a round-robin recording of ideas similar to that used in formal brainstorming. Which method of "getting the ideas" you choose will depend on your group and its needs.)

5. Collect and shuffle cards for anonymity.
6. Ask for volunteers to write entries on chart paper, one person per sheet. Give all volunteers the same color marker (preferably dark—save the colored markers for part two).
   - No talking.
   - No more than six ideas per sheet, evenly spaced, with about six to eight inches between entries.
   - Do not number ideas.
   - Establish a six-inch left margin and draw a bullet on that margin at the beginning of each entry.
   - Absolutely no editing. Write each entry exactly as written on card, including spelling and/or syntax errors.
   - Be neat.
7. Ask volunteer recorders to return cards and markers to the facilitator.
8. Participants should read entries as they are being written on the sheets, search for surprising ideas, and try to think of additional items that are inspired by what they are reading. Write any newly inspired ideas on a sheet of paper for later entry.

## NOMINAL GROUP TECHNIQUE: PART TWO

1. Take each idea in turn and make certain that there is agreement and understanding about what each item means and entails.
2. The team will now vote to reduce the initial list to rank-ordered smaller lists that they can discuss as a group. Each participant should rank order the five ideas/solutions that he or she feels are the most important. The most important idea receives a 5, the next a 4, and so on. Unranked items receive a zero.
3. Develop a chart to record the scores of each group member for his or her five most important ideas. Participants can verbally give their rankings to the chair, who will record them on the chart.
4. In a larger group you may prefer to use the following method of ranking. Give each participant five 3 × 5 cards (seven if the list is very long). Ask participants to select the five most important items and write them out in the center of each card, one item per card. They should then write the item's sequence number in the upper-left corner. While they are doing this, prepare a tally sheet to record the votes by writing as many numbers as there are items under consideration in the voting.

Give participants a four-minute time limit for choosing and writing their five items. When everyone has completed this task, give the following instructions:
- Spread the cards out in front of you so that you can see all five at once. Decide which card is more important than all the others. Write 5 in the lower-right-hand corner and underline it three times. Turn the card over.
- Which is the least important of the four remaining cards? Write 1 in the lower-right-hand corner and underline it three times. Turn the card over.
- Select the most important of the three remaining cards. Write 4 in the lower-right corner and underline it three times. Turn the card over.
- Select the least important of the two cards that are left. Write 2 in the lower-right corner and underline it three times.
- Write 3 in the lower-right-hand corner of the last card and underline it three times.

**5.** Collect the cards. They may be shuffled to communicate to the participants that their voting will be anonymous.

**6.** Ask someone to assist you in reading off the votes or in recording the numbers. The reason the rankings are underlined is to keep you from confusing them with the item numbers.

**7.** Discuss the voting pattern.

**8.** Determine the highest ranked ideas/solutions and what action will be taken on the items.

Materials for the Nominal Group Technique were adapted from *Discussing and Deciding* by Scheidel and Crowell, New York: Macmillan Publishing Co., 1979; *Teaming for Quality Improvement* by H. D. Shuster, Englewood Cliffs, New Jersey: Prentice Hall, 1990; and *Group Techniques for Idea Building* by Carl M. Moore, Newbury Park, California: Sage Publications, 1987.

**PROCESS NUMBER**  **PROBLEM SOLVING**

# FORCE FIELD ANALYSIS

## DESCRIPTION

Force Field Analysis is a problem-solving process developed by Kurt Lewin in the 1940s. Participants identify a problem and then describe the driving forces that will push toward a solution of the problem and the restraining forces that will work against solving the problem.

## APPLICATION

When a situation or problem has been defined or a solution or plan of action has been determined, Force Field Analysis encourages group members to verbalize both positive and negative feelings about the situation or the proposed solution. Identification of positive forces enables group members to capitalize and strengthen these forces, and verbalization of the "negatives" illuminates erroneous information and issues that may be hindering the accomplishment of goals. Force Field Analysis always works best when it involves the group members who are most resistant to change and enlists them in solving the problems.

## ■ TIME REQUIRED
One hour to ninety minutes.

## ■ GROUP SIZE
Five to thirty-five participants.

## ■ MATERIALS
Chart paper, colored markers, pushpins or masking tape. Copies of the Force Field Analysis Worksheet or overhead facsimile.

## ■ PROCESS

1. Put a copy of the diagram shown on the worksheet on a board or chart paper. The copy provided in this book has been completed as an example.

2. Develop a list of "facilitating" (positive or driving) forces that will help the team to solve the problem. Answer the question: What forces will help us to make the needed change? If a force appears to be complex, break it down into its separate components, if possible. At this point, do not worry about which forces are more important.

3. Then develop a list of "restraining" (negative) forces (include as many as you can think of) that will get in the way of a solution or achievement of a goal. Answer the question: What forces will try to stop change from occurring? Again, do not worry about which ones are more important.

4. Rank the restraining forces, agreeing on two or three of them that are most important. Rate these for their solvability. Do not waste time focusing on unsolvable problems ("unalterable variables" as they are called by Benjamin Bloom).

5. For each restraining force you have listed as important, list some possible action steps that you might be able to carry out that would reduce the effect of the force or eliminate it completely.

6. You may now review the action steps you have listed, circle those you intend to do, and move to an action plan immediately, or you may defer that to another meeting.

Process originally developed by Kurt Lewin in conjunction with the National Training Labs in Bethel, Maine, during the 1940s. This adaption taken from the following: Dr. Nicholas DeLuca, Northern Illinois University, May 1980; Dr. Wilma Smith, Illinois Administrator's Academy, January 1990; and *The Second Handbook of Organization Development* by R. A. Schmuck et al., Center for Educational Policy and Management, 1977.

# FORCE FIELD ANALYSIS WORKSHEET

## Cohesive, Effective, Productive Administrative Team

| Facilitating Forces → | ← Restraining Forces |
|---|---|
| Administrative communication/rapport | Money/salary, administrative turnover |
| Clear-cut goals | Board's practice of hiring new superintendent without administrative team input |
| Good interpersonal relations, loyalty to one another and the district | No long-range plan |
| Ability to disagree | Competition for limited resources, recognition, good staff |
| Freedom to do your job and try new ideas | Minimal time to meet |
| Lines of communication are open | Discrepancies in school climate |
| Rich administrative experience making a strong team | Board/administrative split |
| Talented people | Maintenance |
| Physical proximity | |
| Retreat and other opportunities to meet | |
| Resourceful with little money | |

# PROCESS NUMBER 3  PROBLEM SOLVING

# AFFINITY PROCESS

### ■ DESCRIPTION

The Affinity Process is a converging process in which groups take a wide variety of problem issues and group them under agreed-upon headers using "sticky notes." They then determine cause-and-effect relationships between the four headers.

### ■ APPLICATION

This process is especially useful when a group needs to identify the major influences or causes of a problem within a system. Group members may frequently complain about forces that are inhibiting successful program implementation, forces that may not be the real problem. The Affinity Process helps a relatively large group (thirty-five to fifty) to clarify the problem and to determine the real cause of concern. The process precedes the generation of solutions to the problem and avoids time wasted resolving secondary concerns.

### ■ TIME REQUIRED

One hour to ninety minutes.

### ■ GROUP SIZE

Twenty-five to fifty participants.

### ■ MATERIALS

Chart paper, colored markers, sticky notes (such as Post-it™ Notes).

### ■ PROCESS

1. Survey all group members in advance to elicit all problems/concerns.
2. Write each survey item frequently mentioned as a concern on a sticky note (one complete set for each subgroup). There may be as many as twenty or thirty items.
3. Divide the large group into subgroups of from four to six members.
4. Appoint a facilitator for each group.
5. Each group will cluster the ideas/concerns into four groups fitting under a title or header. The copy provided in this book has been completed as a sample. All members of the group must agree on the four headings.
6. Using a large piece of chart paper, each group will then place the four "headers" in a diamond shape (see diagram).
7. The group will then decide how the headers impact each other, determine the cause-and-effect influence, and draw arrows from the causes to the effects (e.g., in the sample, New Staffing Concerns does not impact the other three

headers, so no arrows are drawn from this header to any other. The header that causes the most concern in this example is the Paradigm Shift).

**8.** The groups then share their results.

This process was adapted by Phyllis O'Connell and Nancy Luenzann from materials prepared by Dr. Michael Slusher, CASE Institute, Wheaton, Illinois, January 1992.

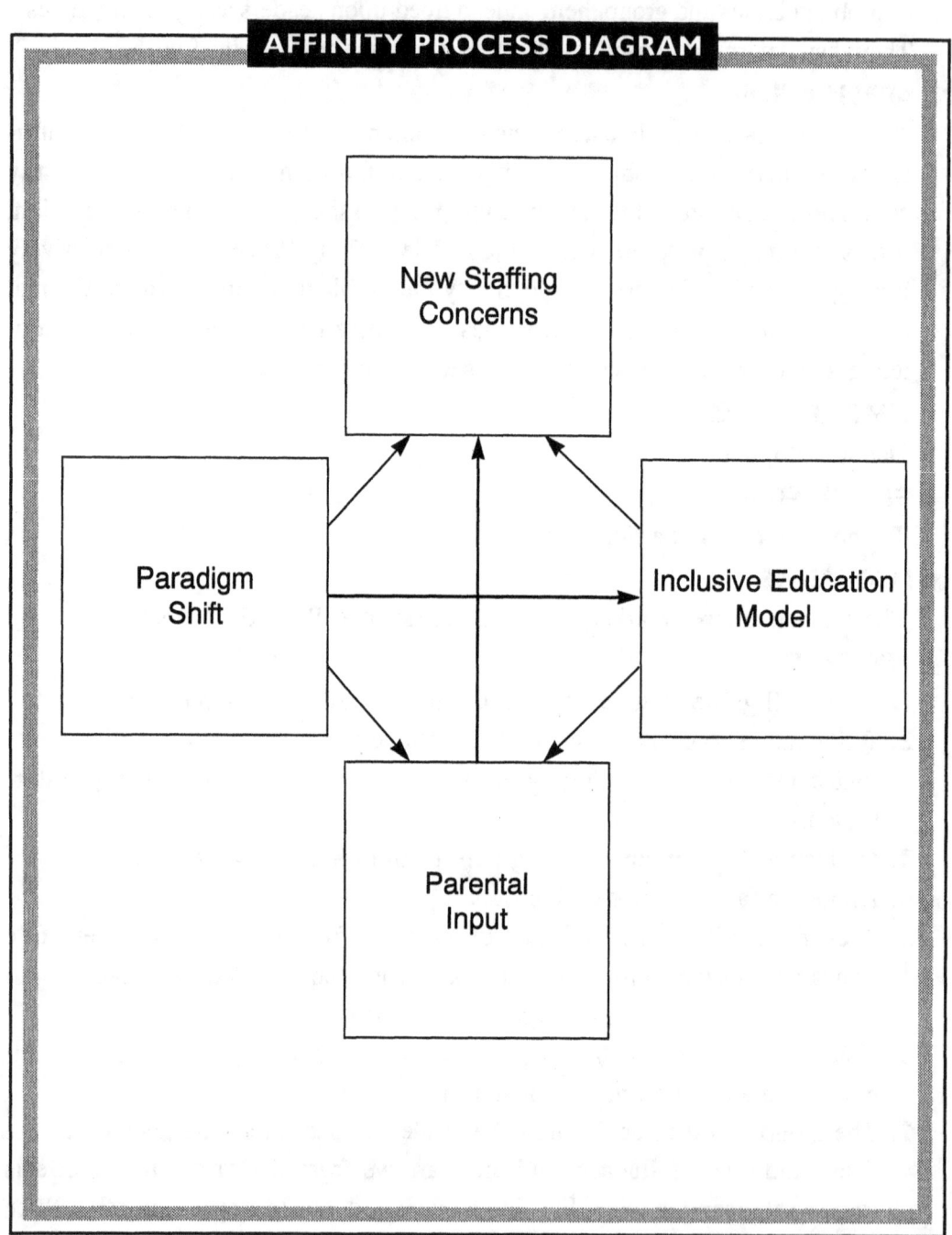

**AFFINITY PROCESS DIAGRAM**

104

**PROCESS NUMBER 4  PROBLEM SOLVING**

# FISHBONE (CAUSE AND EFFECT/ISHIKAWA) DIAGRAM

## ■ DESCRIPTION

The Fishbone Diagram (also known as the Cause and Effect Diagram or the Ishikawa Diagram after the Japanese businessman who invented it) helps teams to identify relationships between causes and effects and get to the bottom of a problem. A fish diagram, which gives the process its name, helps participants to focus on multiple causes (written on the bones of the internal skeletal structure of the fish) of the main problem (written on the head of the fish).

## ■ APPLICATION

This process can be used effectively in the second step of problem solving when teams are trying to identify the causes of a problem that has already been clearly defined.

## ■ TIME REQUIRED

Sixty to ninety minutes.

## ■ GROUP SIZE

Seven to twenty participants.

## ■ MATERIALS

Chart paper and colored markers, pushpins or masking tape.

## ■ PROCESS

1. Draw the fishbone diagram on chart paper (the head of the fish is always on the right-hand side of the page) and write the problem/symptom in the head of the fish. As one's eye moves naturally from left to right, one moves from the causes to the effect. If you prefer, the Modified Fishbone Diagram can be used (see diagram).

2. If needed, pre-establish four or five categories that will stimulate the team's thinking about root causes. The bones of the fish should then be labeled with these categories. Possible categories can always include: People, Materials, Methods, Policy, Technology, or Process. The team, however, can also generate these categories before the process begins. The number of fishbones (lines or categories) is only limited by your team's endurance, expertise, and knowledge. Your fish may grow larger (as fish often do). Just tape up another piece of chart paper to accommodate its growth.

3. Use multi-voting or some other convergent process to narrow the list to the most probable causes.

4. Once you have isolated four to six probable causes for a problem, move to developing a plan for solving the problem.

This process adapted from *Teaming for Quality Improvement* by H. D. Shuster, Englewood Cliffs, New Jersey: Prentice Hall, 1990.

## MODIFIED FISHBONE DIAGRAM

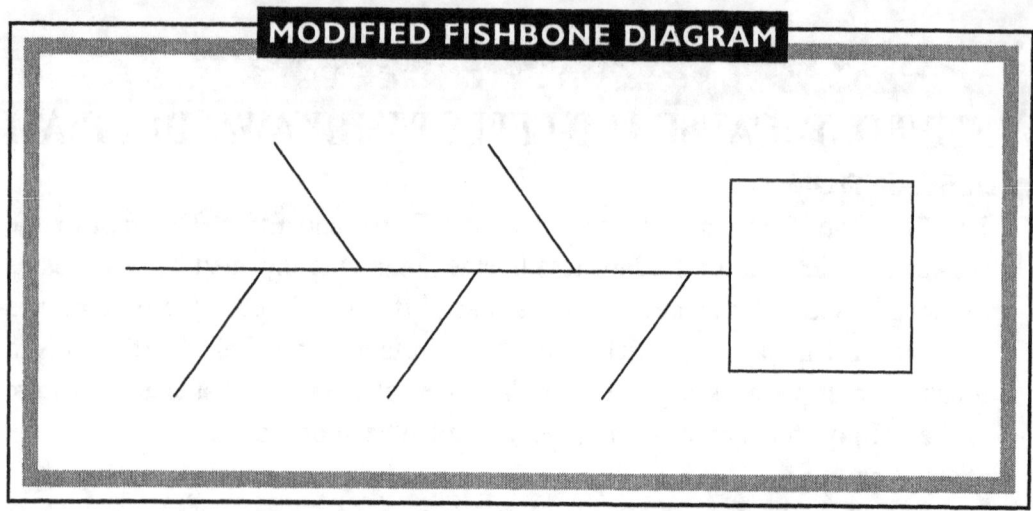

SOURCE: From Shuster, H. David, *Teaming for Quality Improvements: A Process for Innovation and Consensus.* Englewood Cliffs, NJ: Prentice Hall. Copyright © 1990. Reprinted by permission of author.

PROCESS NUMBER **5** PROBLEM SOLVING

# WOTS UP ANALYSIS

### ■ DESCRIPTION

The WOTS Up Analysis gets its name from the four words that produce the WOTS acronym: weaknesses, opportunities, threats, and strengths. Having a clear understanding of these four aspects of an organization will help teams determine the critical problems to be solved.

### ■ APPLICATION

This process is an easy way to conduct a situation audit regarding the state of an institution or organization using the input from a large group of people. The information gathered in the audit can then be used by a planning team to problem solve and plan.

### ■ TIME REQUIRED

Individuals will complete the WOTS Up form in private (fifteen to thirty minutes). A small leadership group will need sixty to ninety minutes to collate and discuss the findings.

### ■ GROUP SIZE

Twenty-five to fifty members can complete the questionnaire. A team of five to ten should collate, discuss, and process the results.

### ■ MATERIALS

Copy of WOTS Up Planning Form for each participant. Chart paper and colored markers to collate the results.

## PROCESS

1. Introduce the WOTS Up Planning Form and distribute it in a large group meeting. Explain the reasons you are gathering the information (to help in goal setting for the coming year, to determine the strengths and weaknesses of our school, etc.). Discuss what is meant by the four categories (Weaknesses, Opportunities, Threats, and Strengths).

2. Identify three or four trusted members of the group (they may be members of the leadership or school management team) to collect the questionnaires. Meet with the team to collate the results. Determine if there is consensus on the major opportunities, threats, strengths, and weaknesses. If sufficient consensus exists, there may be no need to return to the large group until a proposal for seizing opportunities, minimizing threats, maximizing strengths, and strengthening weaknesses has been developed. If, however, after collating the results, there is great divergence, then return to the large group and conduct an affinity process or some other consensus-building process to bring focus to where you will begin in your efforts to effect change and improvement.

<small>This process adapted from materials in "Improving Principals' Performance Through Training in the Decision Sciences" by Harvey J. Brightman, *Educational Leadership*, 41, no. 5, 50–56.</small>

### WOTS UP PLANNING FORM

What are the major WEAKNESSES of our school?

What are the major OPPORTUNITIES available to our school?

What are the major THREATS facing our school?

What are the major STRENGTHS of our school?

## PROCESS NUMBER 6 — PROBLEMS SOLVING

# WHY?-BECAUSE PURSUIT

### ■ DESCRIPTION
The Why?-Because Pursuit is a more restrictive variation of the Fishbone Diagram. Rather than letting participants throw out causes in a free-wheeling manner, the Why?-Because Pursuit insists that a logical linkage be made between each entry. The object is to pursue the cause of something to its very beginnings.

### ■ APPLICATION
Use this process when you have already "fishboned" a variety of causes and now wish to get at one specific cause in greater depth.

### ■ TIME REQUIRED
One hour to ninety minutes.

### ■ GROUP SIZE
Five to twenty-five participants.

### ■ MATERIALS
Chart paper or butcher paper, colored markers, pushpins or masking tape.

### ■ PROCESS
1. Begin with a large piece of blank paper on which the cause statement has been written in a box on the far left middle (see diagram).
2. Go around the group and ask each individual to respond to the question "Why?" On the lines to the right of the cause box, write the "Because" statements. Encourage group members to focus on three or four main statements. If more statements keep coming up, then members are not really ready for this process—they are still doing the fishbone diagram. Continue the process horizontally asking the same "Why?" question and writing the "Because" statements.
3. Number the statements top-to-bottom, left-to-right.
4. Begin combining statements in a vertical fashion in an attempt to reach convergence or consensus. Do not make the mistake of collapsing the diagram horizontally because you will be combining causes and effects.

<sub>Used by permission of the author from *Teaming for Quality Improvement: A Process for Innovation and Consensus* by H. David Shuster, Englewood Cliffs, New Jersey: Prentice Hall, 1990.</sub>

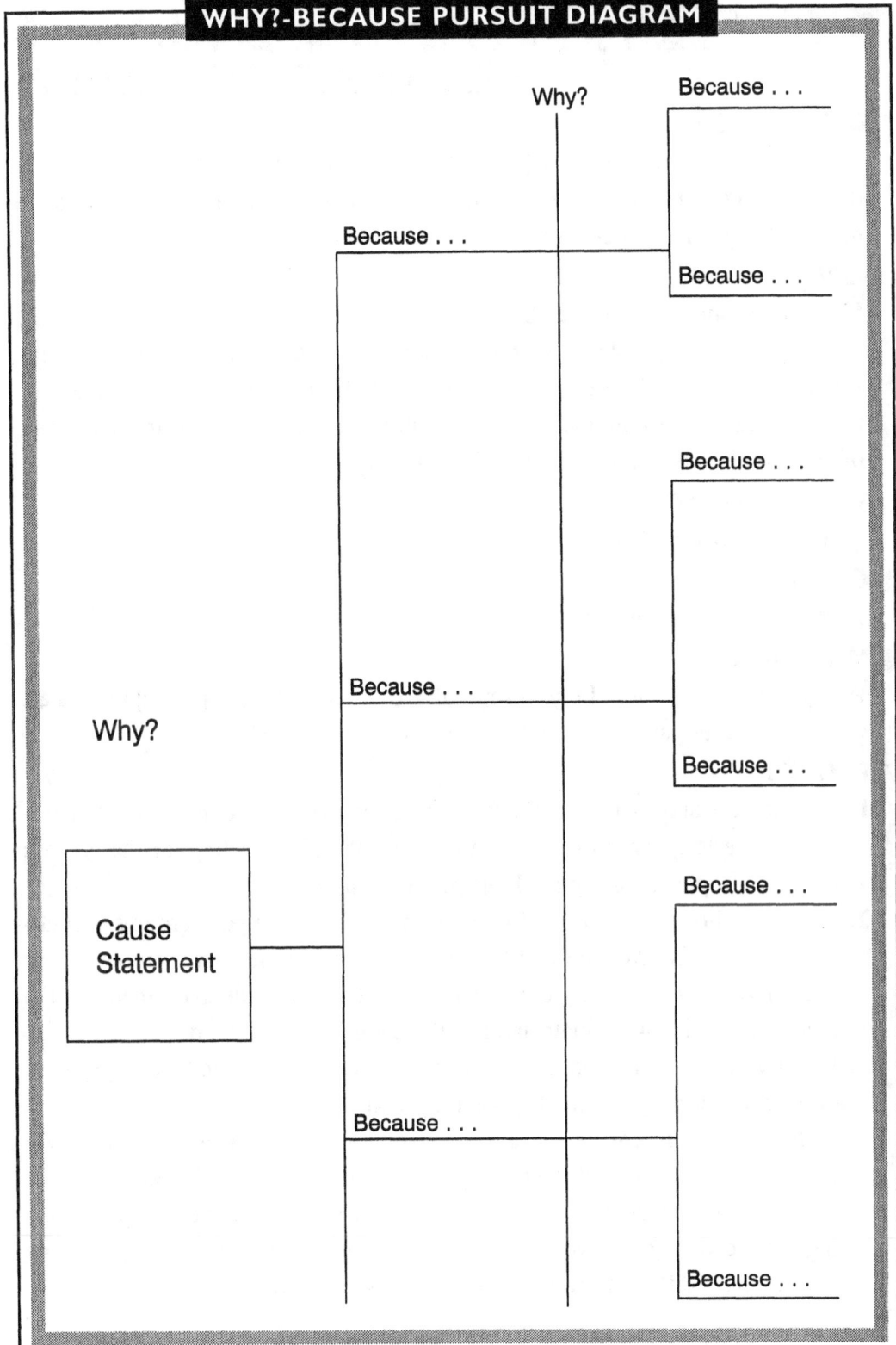

Used by permission of the author from *Teaming for Quality Improvement: A Process for Innovation and Consensus* by H. David Shuster, Englewood Cliffs, New Jersey: Prentice Hall, 1990.

## PROCESS NUMBER 7 — PROBLEM SOLVING

# SITUATION-TARGET-PROPOSAL

### ■ DESCRIPTION

The Situation-Target-Proposal (STP) is a technique that permits participants to define the problem, define the ideal that they believe should exist (in contrast to the situation), and further state their personal idea for solving the problem.

### ■ APPLICATION

If problems and opportunities have not been identified and if some individuals in the group already have ideas about what needs to be done, this process is ideal for getting everyone's agenda out on the table. This process can also be useful for showing a group the variety of perceptions that exist. Group members can often be oblivious to how others feel about key issues.

### ■ TIME REQUIRED

Sixty to ninety minutes.

### ■ GROUP SIZE

Fifteen to fifty participants.

### ■ MATERIALS

A copy of the Situation-Target-Proposal Worksheet for each participant. Chart paper or butcher paper, colored markers, pushpins or masking tape.

### ■ PROCESS

1. This process may be used in the form of a survey or questionnaire for all members of the large group to complete in advance of a meeting, or the process may be completed during the large-group session.
2. Make the choice as to which format to follow based on your group's willingness to share information and be open in front of others. If there are many vocal members and many others who are reticent to volunteer, then use the prequestionnaire and collate and summarize them beforehand.
3. Either way, list each situation/target/proposal that is generated on large pieces of chart paper hung around the meeting room.
4. If the items were collated in advance, some combining and collapsing will already have occurred. If items are suggested from the floor by individuals or small groups, the recorder will need to do some combining and collapsing during the meeting (e.g., two individuals may suggest the same target, but may have entirely different proposals to offer as solutions).

# SITUATION-TARGET-PROPOSAL WORKSHEET

**SITUATION**
What's the problem?

**TARGET**
What's the goal?

**PROPOSAL**
How shall we do it?

**5.** Once all of the STPs have been brought forward to the group, a consensus process should be used to select those to be implemented.

**6.** If a small team has collated the items, the large group can use a consensus process to select one or two. If the large group has generated a variety of ideas, the small team can use the consensus process.

<small>This process adapted from materials prepared by Dr. Wilma Smith, Illinois Principals Association presentation, January 1990.</small>

---

[1] R. Lynch and T. J. Werner, *Continuous Improvement,* (Atlanta, Georgia: QualTeam, Inc., 1992), 160.
[2] Ibid.

## CHAPTER SEVEN

# Group Processes for Reaching Consensus

**WHAT IS CONSENSUS?**

**WHAT ARE SOME IMPORTANT GUIDELINES/GROUND RULES FOR CONSENSUS DECISION MAKING?**

**WHY IS CONSENSUS SO VALUABLE FOR TEAMS?**

**IS THERE A PLACE FOR VOTING AND RANKING IN THE CONSENSUS DECISION-MAKING PROCESS?**

**WHAT PROCESS ACTIVITIES CAN HELP PROMOTE CONSENSUS DECISION MAKING?**

## What is consensus?

Consensus is a much misunderstood form of decision making. Many people think that when you achieve consensus, everyone has agreed. Such is not the case. Consensus is a process whereby group members agree that they can "live with" a decision. Once that agreement has been made, there is a commitment to support the agreement. So consensus is both a process and a goal. The misunderstanding of this concept by the group participants can leave everyone disillusioned about the magic of consensus decision making.

Before deciding that the consensus decision-making process will be used, ask yourself the following key questions:

- Is there a level of trust in our group that allows honesty, directness, and candor? If group members are into game playing, or hold back their feelings out of fear or apathy, consensus will not effective.

- Does the group have a healthy interaction style that allows for open disagreement and does not facilitate or condone dominating and manipulating behaviors?

- Is the leader just one of the group members? If the leader totally dominates the group, then consensus decision making will be a farce. The leader of a consensus decision-making group must be able to tolerate conflict, ambiguity, controversy, temporary stalemates, and shifts of opinions.

- Does the group have adequate time available to engage in consensus decision making? If time is not available, it will drive the process too hastily.

- Are all group members equally well informed about the critical issues so they can participate in the process intelligently? If members are ill informed, the consensus decision process cannot be effective.

> If consensus is to be used effectively, all group members must contribute their views on the issue and their reactions to proposed alternatives for group action; no one should be allowed to remain silent.
>
> —David W. Johnson and Frank P. Johnson

## What are some important guidelines/ground rules for consensus decision making?

Even if all of the above-mentioned conditions exist, you aren't home free. There are some important ground rules for each group member to keep in mind:

- Avoid arguing blindly for your own position. Present your position as clearly and logically as possible, but listen to other members' directions and consider them carefully before you press your point.

- Avoid changing your mind only to reach agreement and avoid conflict. Support only solutions with which you are at least somewhat able to agree. Yield only to positions that have objective and logically sound foundations.

- Avoid conflict-reducing procedures such as majority voting, tossing a coin, averaging, and bargaining.

- Seek out differences of opinion. They are natural and expected. Try to involve everyone in the decision process. Disagreements can improve the group's decision because they present a wide range of information and opinions, thereby creating a better chance for the group to hit upon more adequate solutions.

- Do not assume that someone must win and someone must lose when discussion reaches a stalemate. Instead, look for the next more acceptable alternative for all members.
- Discuss underlying assumptions, listen carefully to one another, and encourage the participation of all members.[1]

## Why is consensus so valuable for teams?

There are easier and faster ways to make decisions, but consensus decision making has its unique advantages for a team.

- Consensus decision making changes behaviors and attitudes. It has been said that "the process is more important than the product," and what happens to individuals as they participate in consensus decision making can often be magical. There is a synergy that takes place during consensus decision making that somehow transforms the individual members of the group as they learn how to listen, gain the ability to give and take, and begin to compromise and consider the other person's point of view.
- Consensus decision making increases group buy-in. Individuals who were naysayers and backstabbers frequently become ardent advocates of a decision because they have participated in each aspect of discussion, advocacy, and argument. When total support is critical for implementation, then consensus decision making is mandatory.
- Consensus decision making improves decision quality. A group product (decision) will by nature of its comprehensiveness be better. Glitches and problems will have been identified and remediated.
- Consensus decision making empowers team members. Participants in consensus decision making (if done right) will feel a new sense of ownership,

---

Where Are We In the Process? Let's Talk About It

What are our points of agreement?

What are our points of disagreement?

Where do we have a consensus? a majority? a hung jury?

Are we differing because we have:
- different goals or pressures?
- different experiences?
- different values?
- "hot buttons" (certain words or concepts that prompt us to argue and become defensive)?
- polarized into adversarial caricatures of ourselves ("the whole language" vs. "the basal advocates")?

—Adapted from Robert F. Lynch and Thomas J. Werner

responsibility, and motivation for the life and activities of the organization. They will truly care about what happens and will be willing to be held accountable. When there is no opportunity for consensus decision making on the part of a group, there is reduced empowerment, lack of unity, distrust, lack of goal focus, communication breakdowns, and a less productive use of human and material resources. Consensus decision making builds a feeling of "team," gives members ground rules for problem solving, provides for better communication, and gets things done effectively.

## Is there a place for voting and ranking in the consensus decision-making process?

Voting and ranking have their place in consensus decision making; a voting process can reveal such an unusual degree of unanimity that there may be no need for a lengthy consensus decision-making process. Ranking can help eliminate unproductive or unnecessary options, thus shortening the consensus decision-making process. I have chosen to include some ranking processes in this chapter on consensus decision making because of the role it can play at points in the consensus decision-making process. Be clear, however, that voting and ranking in and of themselves are not consensus decision-making processes. If critical decisions are always made through a formal ballot process with a specific cut-off (e.g., 75 percent of the total number of people eligible to vote must vote yes in order to pass a proposal), the 25 percent of the group that decided not to vote ("If I don't vote then I don't have to support the issue") or voted no, has no obligation or commitment to support the decision when it is implemented.

## What process activities can help promote consensus decision making?

The following process activities are designed to help your team reach decisions by consensus. They will give team members structured opportunities to express disagreement, solicit input from even the most recalcitrant team member, and enable all team members to feel that everyone has had a part in the decision.

Each process will contain six parts: 1. Description, 2. Application, 3. Time Required, 4. Group Size, 5. Materials, and 6. Process.

## PROCESS NUMBER 1  ACHIEVING CONSENSUS

# APOLLO PROCESS

### ■ DESCRIPTION

The Apollo Process is a consensus activity that enables group members to synthesize their diverse ideas into one. All members of the group have an opportunity to contribute their thoughts. As a result, support for the final product is usually unanimous.

### ■ APPLICATION

The Apollo Process is especially useful for developing a mission or vision statement, or defining an attribute or quality such as instructional leadership or school effectiveness. Members have an opportunity to develop their own product (definition, summary, etc.) and then look for commonalities with others'.

### ■ TIME REQUIRED

Ninety minutes to two hours.

### ■ GROUP SIZE

Ten to forty participants.

### ■ MATERIALS

Chart paper, markers, masking tape or pushpins. Notepaper and pencil for participants.

### ■ PROCESS

1. Define the task. What idea, goal, or definition must the group agree upon? Include all contingencies. Write the task on chart paper for all to see. A clear statement of the task is critical for this process to succeed.
2. First, ask each person to write his or her own answer to the task. The individual writing task may be done in advance. Having participants write in advance of the workshop is a technique that can be used to save time while also providing participants with the opportunity to think through the task more thoroughly.
3. Then, have each person find/choose/be assigned a partner. Odd-number groups will have one group of three and the rest will be dyads. Each pair of individuals is to produce one product by synthesizing its two definitions or statements into one. Both individuals must support the new product. This will take anywhere from fifteen to forty minutes, depending on the complexity of the task. However, providing ample time will reduce the time needed later on in the process.

4. Once agreement has been reached in the dyads, combine two dyads together and repeat the process of synthesizing the two existing definitions into one that all four people can support. If you have an uneven number of dyads, permit one to be "silent observers" of a chosen foursome. Once that foursome has reached consensus on the task, the silent observers can interact with two speakers from the foursome to combine the foursome product with the dyad product. It is important to combine only two products at a time. Have each foursome put its product on chart paper for use in the next step.

5. Once agreement has been reached in the foursomes, combine them into groups of eight. Resort to the "odd number" procedure referred to in Step 4 should you have an odd number of foursomes. The next task is for eight people to combine two products into one. At this point post the products that have been written on chart paper, and have all eight group members read both products. The purpose of reading both products carefully is to identify areas of agreement between the two products. Select a facilitator for each group of eight to manage the flow of conversation so that all can be heard. The facilitator should encourage each group of eight to identify agreement within the two products. As agreement is identified, the facilitator writes it on a new piece of chart paper (this is the drafting of the new product). All aspects of the definition are worked with in this manner until the group has agreed on the new product.

6. When combining groups of eight to form groups of sixteen, first allow the entire group to read the two definitions that have been posted for all to see. There are several options at this point.
   - Use the facilitator method to work with the group of sixteen in the manner described in Step 5.
   - Use the "fishbowl" technique. Identify four speakers who will do the majority of communicating and seat them in a small circle. Add a fifth chair to the circle but keep it empty. All other group members form a second circle around the foursome. At points during the discussion members of the outer circle may want to contribute to the discussion and they may do so by sitting in the "empty chair." Once they have made their point and are comfortable with the results, they leave the inner circle and return to their outer circle seat.

Materials adapted from Training to Increase Student Achievement workshop, Aurora Chase, West Chicago, IL, August 1985.

**PROCESS NUMBER 2  ACHIEVING CONSENSUS**

# MODIFIED APOLLO PROCESS

## ■ DESCRIPTION

The Modified Apollo Process is a consensus activity that enables a group to synthesize its members' diverse reactions and opinions into a concise list of recommendations. All members of the group have an opportunity to contribute their ideas. As a result, support for the final goal is more likely to be unanimous.

## ■ APPLICATION

The Modified Apollo Process is useful for synthesizing reactions from a large group regarding a proposal or idea. The small groups give individuals an opportunity to express their opinions freely without the constraints that often are present in a large group setting. The views of each group can then be synthesized. The ease with which consensus is reached will enable the leader or team to determine if more process activities are needed.

## ■ TIME REQUIRED

One hour to ninety minutes.

## ■ GROUP SIZE

Ten to forty participants.

## ■ MATERIALS

Chart paper and colored markers.

## ■ PROCESS

1. Team or leadership group presents its recommendation(s) to large group.
2. Large group is randomly divided into groups of three to five members.
3. Members of each group should sit close enough to one another that they can share materials and talk to each other quietly and maintain eye contact with all group members.
4. Each group member should have a different role assigned by the group. Such roles could include summarizer (restates the group's major conclusions or answers), checker (ensures that all members can explain how the answer or conclusion was determined), and encourager (ensures that all members participate actively in the discussion).
5. The group must collaborate to arrive at one decision/recommendation from the group. Ideally all members should be in agreement, and all members should be able to explain the rationale underlying their decision.
6. Each group makes a presentation of its opinions/ideas to the large group.

**7.** After all small groups have reported their decisions and rationales, a general discussion among the entire staff is held.

Modified from the *Apollo Process* by Elaine K. McEwan.

---

### MODIFIED APOLLO PROCESS SAMPLE

**First Draft of Mission Statement:**

The mission of Margaret Mead Junior High is:

To provide a nurturing environment in which students learn to think critically, interact cooperatively, and live responsibly in order to achieve their fullest potential as productive citizens.

To provide a collaborative environment that encourages the building staff to share techniques and philosophies that foster professional development.

To build an alliance among students, parents, teachers, and community that prepares students to assume their role in the 21st century.

**Second Draft of Mission Statement with Revisions Suggested by Small Groups:**

The mission of Margaret Mead Junior High is:

To provide a nurturing **(positive)** environment in which students learn **(a body of knowledge) (need social and emotional growth as well as academic)** to think **(and act)** critically **(also think and act creatively),** interact cooperatively, and live responsibly in order to achieve their fullest potential as productive **(human beings)** citizens **(need fulfillment also).**

To provide a collaborative environment that encourages the building staff to share **(expertise)** techniques and philosophies that foster professional development.

To build an alliance **(promote a partnership)** among students, parents, teachers, and **(members of the)** community that prepares students to assume their role in the 21st century **(or contribute to society from today into the future).**

**Final Draft of Mission Statement Adopted and Supported by the Staff of Margaret Mead Junior High School:**

To provide a nurturing, academic environment in which students learn to think critically and creatively, interact cooperatively, and live responsibly in order to achieve their fullest potential.

To foster a collaborative environment that encourages the building staff to share expertise, techniques and philosophies that enhance professional development.

To promote an alliance among students, parents, teachers, and members of the community that prepares students to contribute to society.

---

SOURCE: Reprinted by permission of the School Leadership Team of Margaret Mead Junior High School, Schaumburg District #54, Schaumburg, Illinois.

# The mission
## of
## Margaret Mead Junior High School
## is

*To* provide a nurturing, academic environment in which students learn to think critically and creatively, interact cooperatively, and live responsibly in order to achieve their fullest potential.

*To* foster a collaborative environment that encourages the building staff to share expertise, techniques and philosophies that enhance professional development.

*To* promote an alliance among students, parents, teachers, and members of the community that prepares students to contribute to society.

SOURCE: Reprinted by permission of the School Leadership Team of Margaret Mead Junior High School, Schaumburg District #54, Schaumburg, Illinois.

## PROCESS NUMBER 3  ACHIEVING CONSENSUS

# THE "HUDDLE" METHOD

### ■ DESCRIPTION
The Huddle Method was developed and popularized by J. Donald Phillips of Michigan State University, and it consists of a division of any group into small groups of four to six members for discussion purposes.

### ■ APPLICATION
This all-purpose method can be used often and adapted readily to a variety of needs. It can be used to tap the total resources of a large group membership in a rather short period of time.

### ■ TIME REQUIRED
Thirty to ninety minutes.

### ■ GROUP SIZE
Six to sixty.

### ■ MATERIALS
Chart paper and markers or overhead projector. Push pins or masking tape.

### ■ PROCESS
1. Write the problem/question/issue on chart paper or an overhead transparency.
2. Divide the group into huddle groups. To divide a smaller group, pass out different kinds of "penny" candy (six pieces of each). Then you can direct all of the people with peanut butter kisses into one group and all those with Mary Janes into another group. Group members can munch on their treats while discussing the problem.
3. Instruct each group to select a facilitator, recorder, and any other roles you may choose.
4. Give the time allowance (at the leader's discretion, depending on time available and complexity of the issue).
5. Move among the groups to be available for questions.
6. If the number of huddles is large or time is short, ask the group to rank ideas or input in order of importance.
7. Huddle groups can report back verbally to the large group or the reports can be collected from each group and a summary prepared.
8. Make sure that all significant points of view are brought before the large group (and discussed) at some point in the future if a written summary was prepared.

Adapted from *Leadership and Dynamic Group Action* by George M. Beal, Joe M. Bohlen, and J. Neil Raudabaugh. Ames, Iowa: The Iowa State University Press, 1962, pp. 191-199.

# PROCESS NUMBER 4 ACHIEVING CONSENSUS

# VIGILANT ANALYSIS

## ■ DESCRIPTION

Crucial to consensus decision making is making sure that all points of view are being considered and that alternative solutions are given "air time." The Vigilant Analysis process is a way to systematically consider all alternatives.

## ■ APPLICATION

When several alternative solutions are being considered, this process ensures that adequate consideration will be given to each solution. When a number of programs (e.g., textbooks) are being considered for program adoption and each is adequate but with a different set of strengths and weaknesses, Vigilant Analysis can be helpful.

## ■ TIME REQUIRED

One to two hours depending on the number of alternatives.

## ■ GROUP SIZE

Ten to thirty participants.

## ■ MATERIALS

Chart paper, colored markers, pushpins or masking tape.

## ■ PROCESS

1. Determine which alternatives will be considered by the process. Clearly define or state them so that all group members understand each of them.
2. Systematically evaluate each alternative on the basis of the following four factors:
   - The tangible gains and losses for the group;
   - The tangible gains and losses for significant others, such as parents and other members of the school district;
   - Large-group self-approval or self-disapproval (Will we feel proud or ashamed if we choose this alternative?); and
   - The approval or disapproval of the decision by significant others (Will important people we are connected with think we made the right decision?).

   This evaluation could take place within small subgroups or within the large-group.
3. Complete a balance sheet for each course of action considered. A balance sheet consists of listing the tangible gains from adopting the alternative on one side and the tangible losses on the other.
4. Rate each gain or loss in terms of its importance on a ten-point scale from "1" (no importance) to "10" (extremely important).

5. After a balance sheet has been completed for each alternative course of action, compare the balance sheets and rank the alternatives from "most desirable" to "least desirable."

6. Determine the next course of action in the consensus decision-making process.

Adapted from Irving L. Janis and Leon Mann, *Decision-Making,* New York: The Free Press, 1977; and David W. Johnson and Roger T. Johnson, *Leading the Cooperative School,* Edina, Minnesota: Interaction Book Company, 1989.

## PROCESS NUMBER 5 — ACHIEVING CONSENSUS

# SECOND-CHANCE MEETING

### ■ DESCRIPTION

A Second-Chance Meeting gives everyone an opportunity to think through all of the consequences of the decision. Second-Chance Meetings help prevent premature consensus and concurrence seeking.

### ■ APPLICATION

When a decision has been made by consensus, and the team or leader senses that tne decision has been made in haste or that some group members have pressured others into "giving in," the Second-Chance Meeting is an ideal opportunity to revisit the issue one last time before a final decision is made.

### ■ TIME REQUIRED

One hour.

### ■ GROUP SIZE

Ten to forty participants.

### ■ MATERIALS

Chart paper and colored markers, pushpins or masking tape.

### ■ PROCESS

1. After consensus has seemingly been reached, announce to the group that a second chance meeting will be held at a specified time for all members to express any remaining doubts or criticisms.

2. Group members then have an opportunity to engage in "safe talk" outside of the meeting. If some staff members need more information, make sure they have it well in advance of the second chance meeting.

3. Convene a second meeting and encourage all members to express any remaining doubts and criticisms about the decision.

4. Take any steps that are needed to solve remaining problems and/or answer questions.

Adapted from David W. Johnson and Roger T. Johnson, *Leading the Cooperative School,* Edina, Minnesota: Interaction Book Company, 1989.

**PROCESS NUMBER 6  ACHIEVING CONSENSUS**

# CONSENSUS BRAINSTORMING

### ■ DESCRIPTION

Consensus Brainstorming is a process for soliciting input from group members in a relatively quick and painless way. The process differs from the brainstorming process used in Chapter Four in that creativity and innovation are not the stated goals.

### ■ APPLICATION

When broad categories of familiar responses are called for, this type of brainstorming can be useful. It is particularly useful when developing a list of items that can be readily accepted by a group (e.g., classroom rules, items to be included on the all-school supply list, questionnaire items for a survey).

### ■ TIME REQUIRED

Forty-five to ninety minutes.

### ■ GROUP SIZE

Five to fifty participants.

### ■ MATERIALS

Chart paper and colored markers, pushpins or masking tape.

### ■ PROCESS

1. Write in clear, concise language the issue for the group to address, such as "What are the books we expect all high school seniors to have read by the time they graduate?"
2. Ask individuals to provide responses. When a response is given, ask, by show of hands, for those who agree with the response. Record the response if at least 20 percent of the group is in agreement.
3. Continue the process until there are no further responses that can obtain 20 percent support.

Adapted from James Slezak, *Odyssey to Excellence,* San Francisco: Merritt Publishing Co., 1984.

**PROCESS NUMBER 7  REACHING CONSENSUS**

# ADVOCACY SUBGROUPS

### ■ DESCRIPTION

The Advocacy Subgroup process provides a forum for two alternative solutions of comparable quality to be adequately considered.

125

## ■ APPLICATION

Use this process when the team is about equally divided on two options. Although your team has carefully researched the options, positions have become entrenched and further information is needed to help the team reach consensus.

## ■ TIME REQUIRED

One hour to ninety minutes.

## ■ GROUP SIZE

Ten to fifty participants.

## ■ MATERIALS

Copies of handout materials that either subgroup may wish to distribute to the other subgroup.

## ■ PROCESS

1. Clearly identify and place in writing, where all group members can see them, the two alternative solutions or choices.
2. Assign team members to advocacy subgroups.
3. Give advocacy subgroups time to prepare their position and supporting rationale.
4. Have each subgroup present and elaborate its position and rationale to the group. Each group should present its information in the same structured format. If one group is using "bells and whistles" for its presentation, then the other group should do so also.
5. Have an open discussion in which subgroups argue their points of view and refute the other positions. Each position should be critically evaluated, with doubts and objections freely expressed. In effect, each subgroup is a "devil's advocate" in criticizing the other positions.
6. An alternative is to have each subgroup present the position or choice to which they do not subscribe. This perspective-reversal can ensure that each subgroup listens carefully to the other presentations and comprehends their rationales completely.
7. Synthesize arguments until a consensus is reached.

Adapted from David W. Johnson and Roger T. Johnson, *Leading the Cooperative School*, Edina, Minnesota: Interaction Book Company, 1989.

## PROCESS NUMBER 8 — ACHIEVING CONSENSUS

# RANKING

### ■ DESCRIPTION
Various types of rankings help group members determine which of many options are worthy of more consideration.

### ■ APPLICATION
Use ranking techniques when you need to narrow a very large list of suggestions/ideas/options to the few that will be considered for action.

### ■ TIME REQUIRED
Thirty to sixty minutes.

### ■ GROUP SIZE
Ten to fifty members.

### ■ MATERIALS
Chart paper, colored markers, 4 × 6 cards, note paper, and pencils.

### ■ PROCESS

1. To **rank by scores,** assign each goal/idea/solution/suggestion points from 1 to 5. One point would indicate a very low value placed on the goal, whereas a five rating would rate it at the highest priority. The values that all respondents give to the goal/idea/solution/suggestion are then averaged. The mean score is assigned to the item to be compared to the mean scores of all of the items under consideration.

    To rank by the **card sort method,** write each goal/idea/solution/suggestion on separate cards. Each participant will need a card for every item under consideration. The participants place their cards in stacks that have been assigned values. Usually three to five piles are used. The cards in the high-value piles are the priority goals. The same process can be followed to reduce the number of goals. When members have completed sorting their cards, each pile can be totalled.

    To rank by the **budget allocation method,** allocate each participant twice the number of points that will be used in the ranking process (e.g., if the scale to be used is a five-point scale, assign each participant ten points). Participants give one to five points for each goal/idea/solution/suggestion that they select. When every participant has used up his or her allotted points, the points for each goal are added, giving a score and a basis for identifying priorities.

2. Allow three to five minutes for discussion of the topics identified as priorities through the ranking process. The scores might be close and not differentiated

sufficiently for consensus. The group also needs to determine how many of the priorities it should undertake.

3. Depending upon the situation, participants may need to rank the group's priority topics and present their reasons. A final list can then be determined using the ranking processes explained above.

## PROCESS NUMBER  ACHIEVING CONSENSUS

# PARKING LOT MEETINGS

### ■ DESCRIPTION

This process legitimatizes a practice that goes on anyhow: not saying what's really on your mind in a meeting (e.g., sitting silently, avoiding eye contact, appearing uptight) and then going out to the parking lot and saying what you really think.

### ■ APPLICATION

Use this process whenever you feel a decision-making meeting is going poorly. If the participants are not speaking openly, if the climate is strained, and if people are weighing everything they say very carefully, then the Parking Lot Meeting will get the issues on the table.

### ■ TIME REQUIRED

Thirty to forty-five minutes.

### ■ GROUP SIZE

Twenty-five to fifty participants.

### ■ MATERIALS

Chart paper and colored markers, pushpins and masking tape.

### ■ PROCESS

1. Either as part of the regular meeting or in a specially assembled Parking Lot Meeting, form participants into parking lot groups of their choice.
2. Describe the concept of parking lot meetings and give them about fifteen to twenty minutes to conduct their meeting. The originator of this concept, John J. Koehn, actually sends group members out to the parking lot (if the weather is nice) to have their meetings.
3. Convene all groups and ask each parking lot group to share the substance of its discussion with the entire group. Select a recorder to list all of the problems/concerns mentioned on chart paper.
4. Deal with the issues that were raised in the parking lot meeting and proceed with other consensus decision-making processes.

Adapted from "Dealing with Hidden Agendas: Try 'Parking Lot Meetings'," by John J. Koehn. *The Developer,* February 1994, No. 3, 3–4.

**PROCESS NUMBER 10  ACHIEVING CONSENSUS**

# DIAMONDS NINE

### ■ DESCRIPTION
The Diamonds Nine process is a quick visual scan of a group's priorities in terms of problems to be solved or approaches to be considered.

### ■ APPLICATION
Use in a small group setting where there are approximately nine options from which to select.

### ■ TIME REQUIRED
Thirty to forty-five minutes.

### ■ GROUP SIZE
Five to fifteen participants.

### ■ MATERIALS
A copy of the Diamonds Nine Display for each participant.

### ■ PROCESS
1. Explain to participants that they will be ranking their priorities on the Diamonds Nine Display sheet.
2. Ask each participant to enter the option that the individual rates as the best of the selections possible in the box at the top of the diamond.
3. Ask each participant to enter the option that the individual rates as the worst of the selections possible in the box at the bottom of the diamond.
4. Ask each participant to alternate placing the next best in the second line from the top (left-hand box), with the next worst in the second line from the bottom (right-hand box).
5. When completed, each diamond should display the participant's priority ranking of the options available in the following fashion:

```
                    One
          Two                 Three
   Four           Five               Six
          Seven               Eight
                    Nine
```

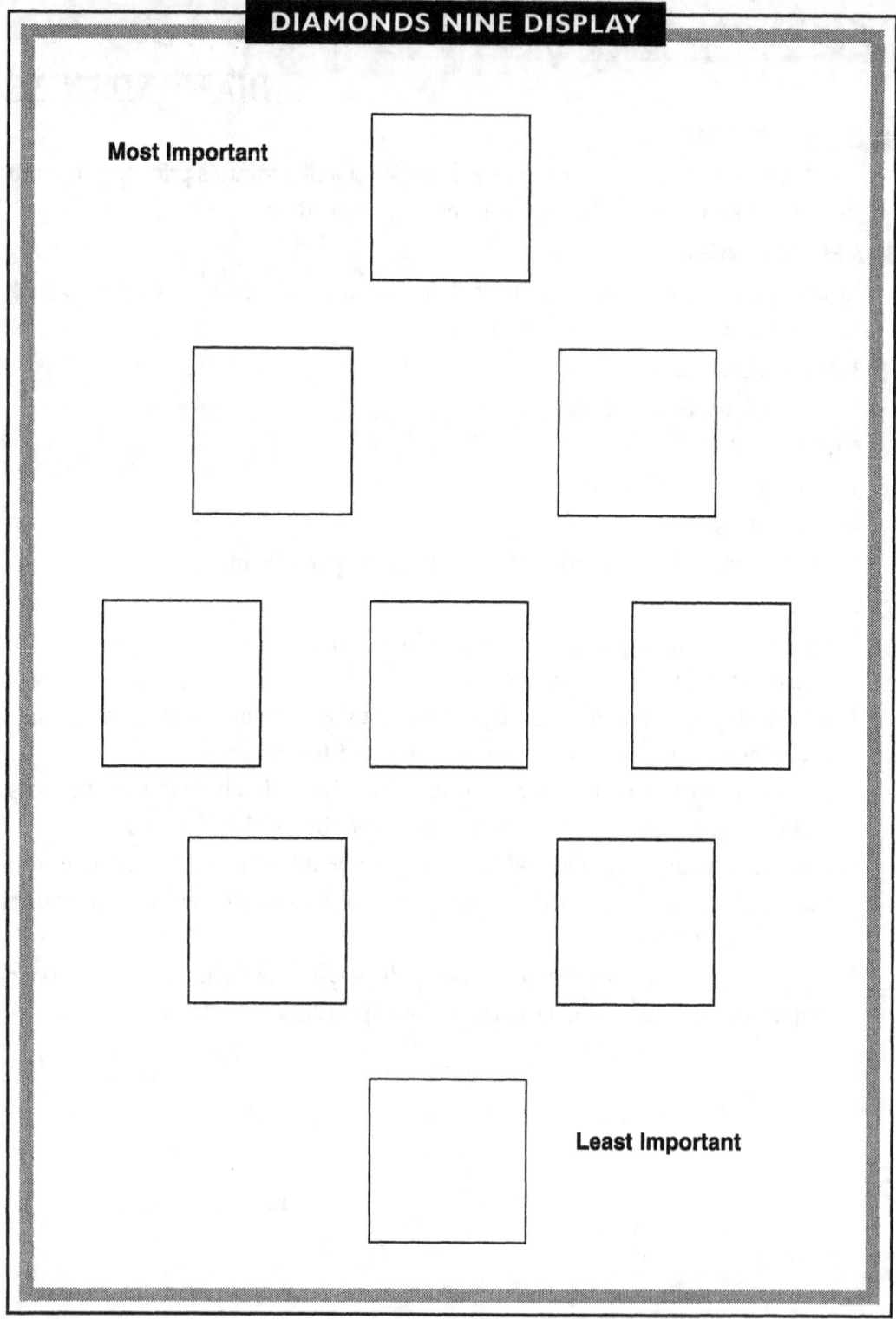

Source: Adapted from materials provided by the New York Education Association.

6. If more than nine options are being considered, add boxes to the center. The real purpose of Diamonds Nine is to discover the top three and bottom three priorities.
7. Ask participants in small groups to place their diamonds in the center of the table and discuss the obvious visual conclusions of the ranking.
8. Discuss and determine next steps.

Source: Adapted from materials provided by the New York Education Association.

## PROCESS NUMBER 11 ACHIEVING CONSENSUS

# MULTIVOTING

### ■ DESCRIPTION
The Multivoting Process is a streamlined way to condense all of your brainstormed/ideas into a short list of the very best.

### ■ APPLICATION
When you have many good ideas, but there is no way the team can consider all of them, Multivoting will enable you to quickly gauge the group's priorities.

### ■ TIME REQUIRED
One hour.

### ■ GROUP SIZE
Ten to twenty-five.

### ■ MATERIALS
Chart paper and colored markers. Push pins or masking tape.

### ■ PROCESS
1. Review the list and combine ideas that are similar.
2. Give each participant a number of votes equivalent to approximately 20% of the total entries that you are considering.
3. Hand out a different color marker to each participant and have them place a mark next to their choices.
4. Delete those items from the list that receive one or no votes, and then repeat the process a second time.
5. Discuss the remaining items in depth to reach a final decision.

Adapted from *Continuous Improvement: Teams and Tools* by Robert F. Lynch and Thomas J. Werner. Atlanta, Georgia: QualTeam, Inc., 1992, p. 169.

**PROCESS NUMBER 12  ACHIEVING CONSENSUS**

# SCANNING STRATEGY

### ■ DESCRIPTION
The Scanning Strategy is designed to "scan" alternatives and eliminate those with serious problems or "crippling" weaknesses.

### ■ APPLICATION
Use the Scanning Strategy when carefully considering all the pros and cons of each possible option.

### ■ TIME REQUIRED
Forty-five to ninety minutes.

### ■ GROUP SIZE
Five to fifteen participants.

### ■ MATERIALS
Chart paper and colored markers; pushpins or masking tape.

### ■ PROCESS
1. List all of the alternatives being considered on chart paper.
2. Examine each alternative and raise as many objections as possible to it. Reject any alternatives that are found to have a "crippling objection."
   Crippling objections could be any of the following:
   - Utilitarian objections: the means required to implement the alternative are not available (e.g., money, human resources, space).
   - Normative objections: implementing the alternative would violate the basic values of the decision makers (e.g., eliminating programs and services to high-risk students).
   - Political objections: implementing the alternative would violate the basic values or interests of a group or individual whose support is essential for implementing the decision and making it work (e.g., support of school board members is crucial and the alternative would not be supported by the majority of them).
3. Use the three-step process (utilitarian objections, normative objections, political objections) with the remaining alternatives.
4. Repeat the process again in still greater detail. On each scanning, the same criteria are applied in increasingly greater detail.

This process adapted from material in *The Active Society: A Theory of Societal and Political Processes* by Amitai Etzioni, New York: The Free Press, 1986; and *Discussing and Deciding* by Scheidel and Crowell, New York: Macmillan Publishing Co., 1979.

## PROCESS NUMBER 13 — ACHIEVING CONSENSUS

# FIST-TO-FIVE

### ■ DESCRIPTION

Fist-to-Five is a quick process for determining how close to consensus a group may be. Participants hold up five fingers for total support and agreement or a fist to indicate total disagreement. There are other choices in between indicated by different numbers of fingers.

### ■ APPLICATION

Use this process any time during discussion or other group processes to determine if agreement may be close.

### ■ TIME REQUIRED

Ten to fifteen minutes.

### ■ GROUP SIZE

Five to twenty-five participants.

### ■ MATERIALS

Chart paper or overhead on which to write the meaning of different combinations of fingers.

### ■ PROCESS

1. Teach group members the following hand signals:
   - Five fingers: Go for it! Five fingers means you wholeheartedly agree with this decision/idea/goal/option and will **be a leader in the implementation process.**
   - Four fingers: I agree and will help. Four fingers means you agree with the decision/idea/goal/option and will do whatever you can to **assist in implementation.**
   - Three fingers: **Agreement with reservation.** Three fingers means I agree but have some doubts about the whole thing. I'm in a total quandary and neutral.
   - Two fingers: **Agreement with reservation and need more clarification.** I will support the proposal.
   - One finger: **Not in total agreement, but I can live with it.** I won't work to block the proposal if adopted, but I'm not going to be totally supportive either.

- Fist raised: **Disagree.** I cannot live with this idea/goal/option, but here is an alternative or a modification that I can live with. If you adopt this proposal, I may have to block it.

2. Display a copy of what each hand signal means where all participants can see it.
3. Clearly state the proposal that is under consideration.
4. Ask for participants to show a "fist to five" to indicate their level of agreement.
5. Pay special attention to the participants who showed one fingers, two fingers, or a fist. Ask these individuals, "What part of our current proposal do you object to?" Very often, there is one small glitch (more staff development is needed before we can implement; the time lines are too fast; or I'm afraid I will fail) that can be remediated without losing the entire idea.
6. Continue with discussion or other group process.

Adapted from *Odyssey to Excellence* by James Slezak, Millbrae, California: Merritt Publishing Company, 1984.

## Process Number 14 — Achieving Consensus

# SPEND-A-BUCK

### ■ DESCRIPTION
Spend-a-Buck is a unique and enjoyable way for a group to determine the relative importance of approximately five to ten issues. Participants spend a limited amount of imaginary money to "buy" the issues that are of most value to them.

### ■ APPLICATION
Use when you have a list of issues that needs to be reduced to one or two.

### ■ TIME REQUIRED
Thirty to forty-five minutes.

### ■ GROUP SIZE
Ten to fifteen participants.

### ■ MATERIALS
Chart paper, colored markers, pushpins or masking tape, enough 3 × 5 cards for each participant to have one card per item under consideration.

### ■ PROCESS
1. Distribute 3 × 5 cards to participants and have them write one issue on each card.

2. Instruct participants that they have a total of one dollar to spend on the issues according to the issue's relative importance. They must spend a minimum of twenty cents on an item. Instruct them to write the amount they wish to spend on an item on the card.
3. Ask participants to start with their top priorities, then go to their low priorities, and to finish with the middle-valued group.
4. Collect the cards, sort them by issue, and tabulate the total value of each issue.
5. Rank the issues by total value.
6. Analyze the rankings.

<small>Adapted from *Odyssey to Excellence* by James Slezak, Millbrae, California: Merritt Publishing Company, 1984, p. 179.</small>

## PROCESS NUMBER 15 — ACHIEVING CONSENSUS
# PRIORITY MATRIX

### ■ DESCRIPTION
This process is an easy and efficient way to assist groups in prioritizing many options to determine those that are most important.

### ■ APPLICATION
Use this process when you want total participation in a decision and have many options to consider.

### ■ TIME REQUIRED
One hour.

### ■ GROUP SIZE
Fifteen to forty participants.

### ■ MATERIALS
Copy of Priority Matrix for each participant. Chart paper and colored markers to create a large matrix. Overhead transparency of the matrix and overhead pens are optional.

### ■ PROCESS
1. List each of the options in one of the boxes at the top and also in one of the boxes on the left-hand side of the matrix.
2. Lead the group through a consideration of each box by asking the question: Is Option A, the option written on the top, more important than Option B, the option written along the side?

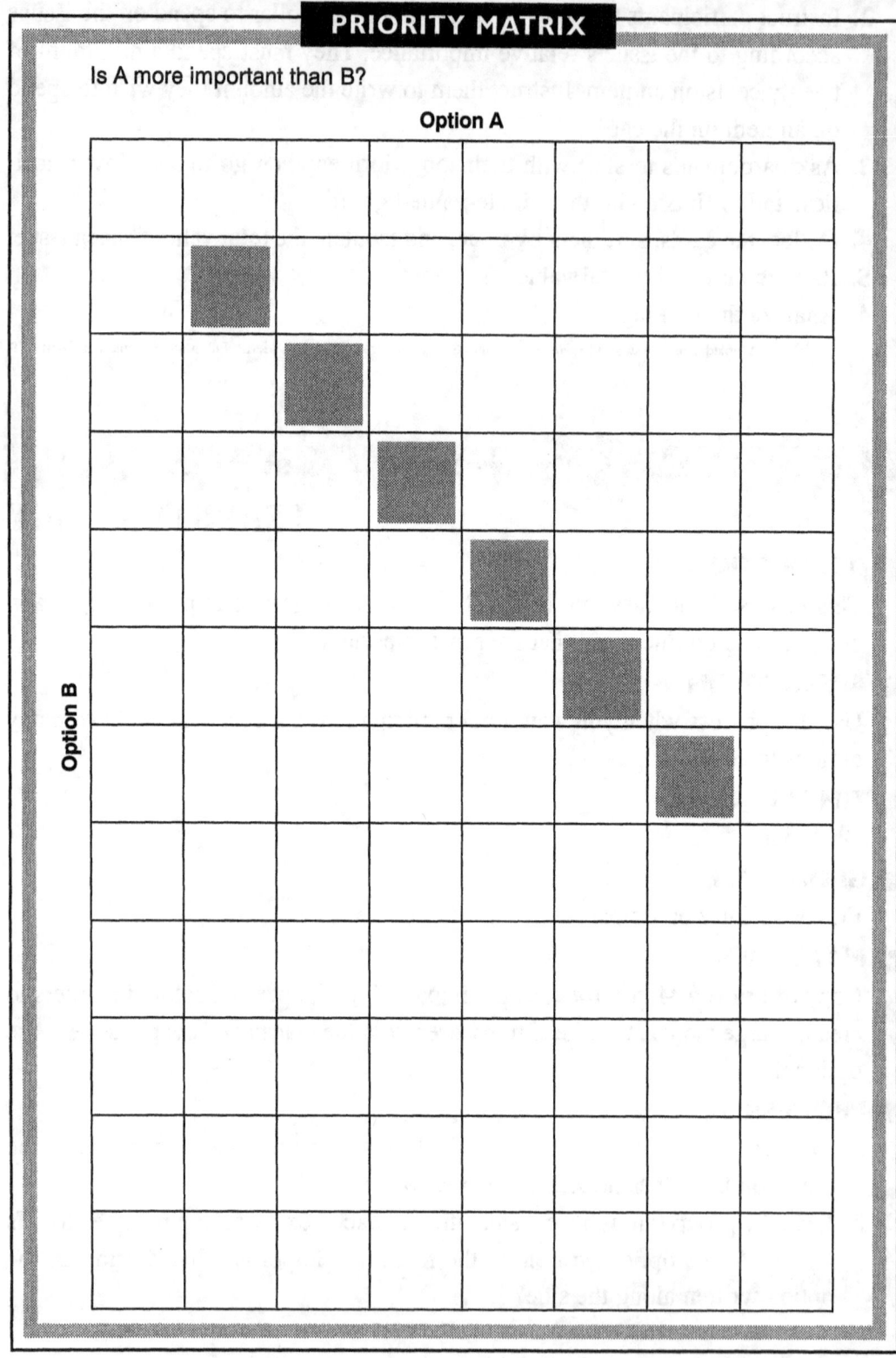

SOURCE: Reprinted by permission of the author, Phyllis O'Connell.

## SAMPLE PRIORITY MATRIX

Is A more important than B in our desire to improve communication/public relations with parents?

**Option A**

|  | Parent Conferences | News Releases | Telephones in Classrooms | Weekly Letters from Teachers | School Newsletter | Open Houses |  |
|---|---|---|---|---|---|---|---|
| Parent Conferences | ■ |  |  |  |  |  |  |
| News Releases |  | ■ |  |  |  |  |  |
| Telephones in Classrooms |  |  | ■ |  |  |  |  |
| Weekly Letters from Teachers |  |  |  | ■ |  |  |  |
| School Newsletter |  |  |  |  | ■ |  |  |
| Open Houses |  |  |  |  |  | ■ |  |
|  |  |  |  |  |  |  |  |
|  |  |  |  |  |  |  |  |
|  |  |  |  |  |  |  |  |
|  |  |  |  |  |  |  |  |
|  |  |  |  |  |  |  |  |

**Option B**

SOURCE: Adapted from the Priority Matrix form developed by Phyllis O'Connell.

3. Place a 0 in the box if the group's answer to the question is no. Place a 1 in the box if the group's answer to the question is yes.
4. The matrix can also be completed by individuals and the scores averaged. This method will insure that everyone's score will be included, but the process will be lengthier than a general discussion.

Developed by and used with permission of Phyllis O'Connell of Renewal Resources, Sandwich, Illinois.

---

[1]D. W. Johnson and F. P. Johnson. *Joining Together* (Englewood Cliffs, New Jersey: Prentice Hall, 1982), 106.

■ CHAPTER EIGHT

# Group Processes for Resolving Conflict

---
**WHAT IS CONFLICT RESOLUTION?**
---
**WHAT KINDS OF CONFLICT CAN INTERFERE WITH QUALITY DECISION MAKING?**
---
**WHAT ATTITUDES ARE ESSENTIAL TO EFFECTIVE CONFLICT RESOLUTION?**
---
**WHAT PROCESS ACTIVITIES CAN HELP PROMOTE CONFLICT RESOLUTION?**

## What is conflict resolution?

The concept of conflict resolution is a popular one today. Curricula are being introduced in schools to teach children at an early age how to achieve consensus regarding an issue without resorting to violence or even argument. Students are practicing on playgrounds and in lunchrooms, and their skills and enthusiasm are a hopeful sign. Competition is out and cooperation is in. But the rise of conflict resolution as a "hot topic" in schools today does not automatically confer upon leaders and group members a ready-made set of these skills. We have not had courses of study or practice in conflict resolution and are learning along with the children. These skills are often achieved the hard way, leaving us exhausted, bloodied, and battered, wondering if the adults with whom we work can be retrained to leave their win-lose and competitive value structure behind when they enter meeting rooms.

## What kinds of conflict can interfere with quality decision making?

There are two kinds of conflict that can occur within your team: conflict that has its origin in the task or assignment that the group is working on and conflict that is related to the individuals involved. The former is much easier to deal with than the latter. When strong interpersonal relationships exist between team members and they like each other, conflict can often be resolved merely with more information, more efficient problem-solving methods, and more involvement by the group leader. However, when there are group members who are argumentative, need to dominate, have hidden agendas, and are emotionally immature, resolving conflicts will be more challenging.

> Most people do not act according to what they know, but according to what they feel about what they know.
> —Rachel Davis DuBois and Mew-Soong Li

## What attitudes are essential to effective conflict resolution?

Effective conflict resolution is absolutely essential to quality decision making. But the playing field has to be level and all participants must subscribe to a similar set of values in order for conflict to be resolved in the course of the decision-making process. And, if you are not encountering conflicts as you solve problems and work together, then you and your team must be sweeping many important issues under the carpet. Conflict is inevitable; it is healthy, and it can be resolved.

If you and your team members can answer "yes" to the following questions, you're ready to resolve conflict and achieve consensus.

> Where the interests of the parties are mutually exclusive—that is, where the gain of one party's goal is at the cost of the other's, or where the parties have different values—then the resulting social interaction between the parties contains fertile ground for conflict.
> —Alan C. Filey

- Do you believe that conflicts can actually be resolved?
- Do you believe that resolving conflicts is a worthy goal?
- Do you believe in cooperation rather than competition?
- Do you believe that everyone on your team is of equal value?
- Do you believe that other team members' statements are accurate views of their positions and that they have a right to change those views in the course of the discussion?
- Do you believe the differences of opinion are helpful?

- Do you believe that your fellow team members are trustworthy?
- Do you believe that team members can compete, but they have chosen to cooperate?

## What process activities can help promote conflict resolution?

The following process activities are designed to help your team resolve conflict. They will give team members simulation opportunities to experience the results of cooperation as opposed to competition, as well as specific techniques to use in the decision-making process when conflicts arise.

> Have you learned lessons only of those who admired you, and were tender with you. And stood aside for you?
> Have you not learned great lessons from those who braced themselves against you, and disputed the passage with you?
> —Walt Whitman, 1860

Each process will contain six parts: 1. Description, 2. Application, 3. Time Required, 4. Group Size, 5. Materials, and 6. Process.

### PROCESS NUMBER 1 — CONFLICT RESOLUTION

## THE GAME OF CHICKEN

### ■ DESCRIPTION

The Game of Chicken is similar to the scene enacted in every teenage rebel Grade B movie. Two adolescents are driving their cars toward one another at high speeds, each with one set of wheels on the center line of the highway. If neither veers, they will crash. Whoever veers is chicken. Both drivers prefer to avoid death, but they also want to avoid the dishonor of being chicken.

### ■ APPLICATION

When groups are having a difficult time with cooperation and collaboration, this process will show them the benefits that can accrue to individuals and groups that choose cooperation.

### ■ TIME REQUIRED

Thirty to sixty minutes.

### ■ GROUP SIZE

Two teams of three to eight persons seated far enough apart so that they cannot overhear or communicate with each other unless told to do so.

### ■ MATERIALS

Tally sheet for each group member. Scoring instructions for each group member.

## PROCESS

1. Divide large group into two subgroups. Pass out instructions and assign groups to their separate locations.
2. Give time for each group member to read the directions silently.
3. After the instructions have been read, review the following instructions with the group.
   - The objective of this exercise is for the team to earn as many points as it can. Drivers A and B (represented by the two subgroups) can make one of two choices in each of the ten rounds of the exercise: Stay on Course or Veer.
   - Example: If Drivers A and B both choose to stay on course, they each lose ten points. If Drivers A and B both choose to veer, they each lose one point. If Driver A chooses to stay on course and B veers, Driver A loses five points and Driver B gains five points. If Driver A chooses to veer and Driver B stays on course, Driver A gains five points, and Driver B loses five points.
   - The outcome depends on what both drivers do, and each driver must try to predict how the other will behave. One or both players may place different values on the outcomes than is suggested by the numbers above. For example, one may prefer death to dishonor. Each player must try to calculate the values of the other, and neither has complete information about the values of his opponent.
   - A key concept in game theory is that of strategy. Strategy is defined as rational decision making in which a set of moves is designed to achieve optimum payoff even after consideration of all of the opponent's possible moves.
   - Another key concept is *minimax*. Minimax refers to the rational strategy that either minimizes the maximum loss or maximizes the minimum gain regardless of what the opponent does. It is designed to protect against your opponent's best play. It is a conservative strategy because it is designed to reduce losses and to ensure minimum gains rather than seek maximum gains at great risk of loss. Minimax is viewed by most game theorists as the most rational choice.
   - The rational player in this game of chicken will veer because his choice minimizes the maximum loss.
4. During each round, subgroup members will have three minutes to determine their choice for the round.

5. After each round, the scorekeeper collects the decision from each subgroup and conveys the total choice to each subgroup for scoring. One scorekeeper should be assigned to each pair of subgroups. He or she will need to keep the groups moving according to the time schedule.
6. After all rounds have been completed, debrief with the groups using questions like: How were decisions made in your team? Who was the most influential member in your team? What were the advantages and disadvantages of collaborating with, competing with, being suspicious of, trusting, defeating, or losing to the other team? How was the way we worked in this process like or unlike everyday life in this organization?

Adapted from lecture and notes of Dr. Nicholas DeLuca, Professor of Educational Administration, Northern Illinois University, May 1980.

## THE GAME OF CHICKEN SCORING SHEET

| ROUNDS | Driver A | Driver B |
| --- | --- | --- |
| Round One | | |
| Round Two | | |
| Round Three | | |
| Round Four | | |
| Round Five | | |
| Round Six | | |
| Round Seven | | |
| Round Eight | | |
| Round Nine | | |
| Round Ten | | |

Drivers A and B both choose to stay on course: Each loses 10 points.
Drivers A and B both choose to veer: Each loses 1 point.
Driver A stays on course and B veers: Driver A loses 5 points and Driver B gains 5 points.
Driver B Stays on course and A veers: Driver B loses 5 points and Driver A gains 5 points.

SOURCE: Handout provided during lecture by Dr. Nicholas DeLuca, Professor of Educational Administration, Northern Illinois University, May 1980.

## PROCESS NUMBER 2 REDUCING CONFLICT

# FISHBOWL STRATEGY

### ■ DESCRIPTION
The Fishbowl Strategy uses a form of representative government to air conflicting points of view.

### ■ APPLICATION
Use this process when a conflict has arisen about two differing sides of an issue.

### ■ TIME REQUIRED
Forty-five to sixty minutes.

### ■ GROUP SIZE
Twenty to forty participants.

### ■ MATERIALS
None.

### ■ PROCESS
1. Choose two representatives, one from each of the divergent sides of the issue.
2. Have these two individuals sit in chairs placed in the center of the room—"The Fishbowl."
3. Add two chairs to this "fishbowl," one for you, the group leader, and one empty chair.
4. Arrange the other members of the group in close proximity to their fishbowl "rep."
5. If a member of the audience wishes to add to the discussion, he or she must come up and sit in the empty chair. Only when the leader recognizes that individual may he or she speak. When he or she has finished, that person returns to the audience area.
6. Move the discussion along at a good pace. After about five minutes, send the representatives back to their subgroups for one to two minutes. The purpose of this time-out is to check on the accuracy and intent of their presentation in the view of their constituents.
7. This process may be repeated several times if desired. Once the conflict has been identified, the group may use another strategy to resolve it.

*Process adapted from presentation by Dr. Wilma Smith on Site-Based Management, Illinois Principals Association, January 1990, St. Charles, Illinois.*

**PROCESS NUMBER 3  RESOLVING CONFLICT**

# COERCING AGREEMENT

## ■ DESCRIPTION

In this process, the leader steps in and uses a structured and organized approach to bring understanding and clarification to a situation that has "gone sour." Although there is no guarantee that this process will bring about consensus or eliminate differences, the structured questioning process helps to reduce tension and sometimes causes a proponent to re-examine and modify or withdraw a proposal.

## ■ APPLICATION

Coercing Agreement is a process to be used only as a last resort when the group cannot agree and when that lack of agreement is causing tension, dissension, and unhealthy conflict.

## ■ TIME REQUIRED

Sixty to ninety minutes.

## ■ GROUP SIZE

Fifteen to forty participants.

## ■ MATERIALS

None.

## ■ PROCESS

1. Explain that as leader you are declaring a time-out period and invoking your privilege and position as leader of the group.
2. Identify a member of the group who is identified with the controversy and ask that individual to state or restate the position. This individual is not to be interrupted with denials or rebuttals. Any interruptions will be ruled out of order.
3. Group members may ask questions of the speaker during this period, but only of three types:
   - To clarify (e.g., What did you mean? Did you say?)
   - To examine uniqueness (e.g., In what ways is this different from what happened last year?)
   - To find means of testing (e.g., Can you give us any way of testing your assumptions or predictions?)
   
   Watch carefully for any statements that are evaluative or confrontative and rule them out of order.
4. Once the period of presentation and questioning has been completed, return to the problem-solving process or discussion that was being used.

This process adapted from "Procedures for Coercing Agreement," by Irving J. Lee, *Harvard Business Review*, 32 (January-February 1954): 39–45; and *Discussing and Deciding* by Scheidel and Crowel, New York: Macmillan Publishing Co., 1979.

# Process Number 4 — Reducing Conflict

## PRISONER'S DILEMMA

### ■ DESCRIPTION

This process simulates a risk-taking situation not unlike that experienced by two guilty prisoners being questioned separately by the police. Each is told what the other has confessed and that a similar confession will get both of them off easier. The prisoner's dilemma is whether to confess. The exercise allows groups to explore win-lose and zero-sum influence situations and dramatizes the merits of collaboration and competition in intergroup relations.

### ■ APPLICATION

When groups are having a difficult time cooperating and collaborating, this process will demonstrate the advantages that can accrue to individuals and groups who choose cooperation.

### ■ TIME REQUIRED

Thirty minutes to one hour.

### ■ GROUP SIZE

Two teams of from three to eight persons seated far enough apart so that they cannot overhear or communicate with each other unless told to do so.

### ■ MATERIALS

Tally sheet for each group member. Scoring instructions for each group member.

### ■ PROCESS

1. Divide large group into two subgroups. Pass out instructions and assign groups to their separate locations.
2. Give time for each group member to read the directions silently.
3. After the instructions have been read, review the following instructions with the group.
   - The objective of this exercise is for the team to earn as many points as it can. Each subgroup can make one of two choices in each of the ten rounds of the exercise: Red Team can choose either A or B and the Blue Team can choose either X or Y. The number of points awarded is dependent upon the combination of one subgroup's choice with the choice made by the other subgroup.
   - Example: If Reds choose A and Blues choose X, both teams win three points; if Reds choose A and Blues choose Y, Reds lose six points and Blues win six; if Reds choose B and Blues choose X, Reds win six and Blues lose six; if Reds choose B and Blues choose Y, both teams lose three points.

- In addition, points won or lost are doubled in the fourth round and quadrupled in the ninth and tenth rounds. Points for each round will be recorded on the score sheet.
- There are three key rules:
  - The members of one subgroup are not to confer with the members of the other subgroup, except through a representative before rounds four and eight. Negotiators will meet for one minute where they cannot be overheard by either team.
  - Each subgroup must agree upon a single choice for each round.
  - One subgroup is not to know the choice of the other subgroup until instructions are given to reveal it.

4. During each round, subgroup members will have three minutes to determine their choice for the round.
5. After each round, the scorekeeper collects the decision from each subgroup and conveys the total choice to each subgroup for scoring. One scorekeeper should be assigned to each pair of subgroups. He or she will need to keep the groups moving according to the time schedule.
6. Before each bonus round, negotiations will take place.
7. Begin round one and proceed with each round according to the directions.
8. After all rounds have been completed, debrief with the groups using questions like: How were decisions made by your team? Who was the most influential member of your team? What were the advantages and disadvantages of collaborating with, competing with, being suspicious of, trusting, defeating, or losing to the other team? How was the way you worked in this process like or unlike everyday life in this organization?

Ronald Hyman offers these points for consideration from his adaptation of the Prisoner's Dilemma:

- Mutual trust arises when people work together to solve a common problem.
- Face-to-face communication is desirable and promotes the development of trust and mutual benefit.
- Group benefit does not necessarily arise in a group when people pursue their own self-interests.
- If a person breaks a cooperative agreement with another person or violates an established feeling of mutual trust, the hurt person feels angry and often is vindictive.
- People have different interpretations of the same directive.
- When people are emotionally charged up, they often do not act in a logical and reasonable way.

- When people understand their situations themselves and the probable consequences of their actions, conditions are favorable for change to occur.

Adapted from the following materials: Lecture by Dr. Nicholas DeLuca, Professor of Educational Administration, Northern Illinois University, May 1980; Ronald T. Hyman, *School Administrator's Staff Development Activities Manual*, Englewood Cliffs, New Jersey: Prentice Hall, 1986; and J. Pfeiffer, (Ed.), *A Handbook of Structured Experiences for Human Relations Training*, San Diego, California: University Associates, 1983.

## TALLY SHEET FOR PRISONER'S DILEMMA

| ROUNDS | REDS | BLUES | |
|---|---|---|---|
| Round One | | | |
| Round Two | | | |
| Round Three | | | |
| Round Four | | | Points Doubled |
| Round Five | | | |
| Round Six | | | |
| Round Seven | | | |
| Round Eight | | | |
| Round Nine | | | Points Quadrupled |
| Round Ten | | | Points Quadrupled |

SOURCE: Handout provided during lecture by Dr. Nicholas DeLuca, Professor of Educational Administration, Northern Illinois University, May 1980.

## SCORING INSTRUCTIONS FOR PRISONER'S DILEMMA

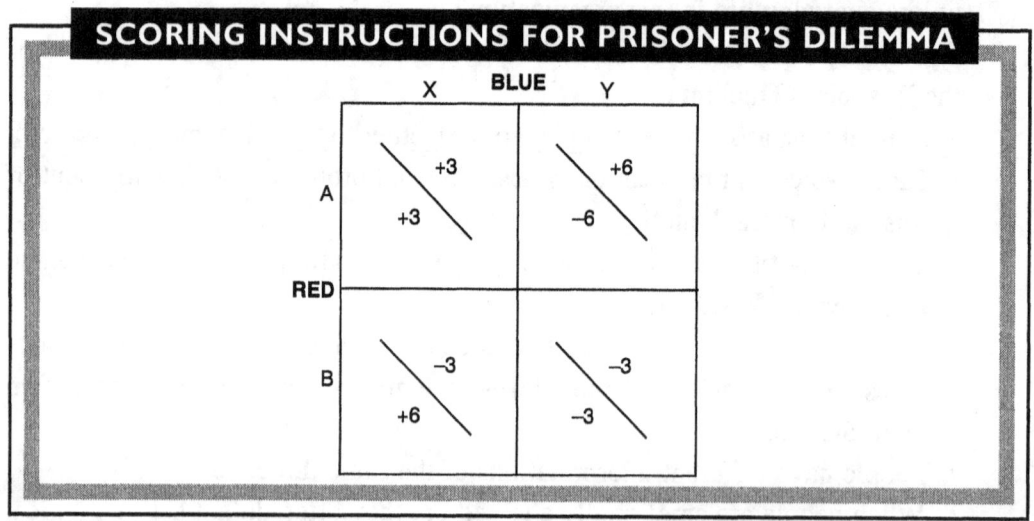

SOURCE: Handout provided during lecture by Dr. Nicholas DeLuca, Professor of Educational Administration, Northern Illinois University, May 1980.

## PROCESS NUMBER 5 — REDUCING CONFLICT

# CONFLICT AND COOPERATION

### ■ DESCRIPTION

This process asks participants in the same group or organization to locate both conflictive and cooperative conditions that can exist in any organization and then to specifically apply that information to their organization or group.

### ■ APPLICATION

Use this process when group members need to be reminded of those conditions in an organization that contribute to conflict or to cooperation. The process accomplishes this goal in a way that minimizes threat and tension since the issues are depersonalized, and since the items are listed on a sheet, there is no identification as to the source of the item.

### ■ TIME REQUIRED

One hour.

### ■ GROUP SIZE

Ten to thirty participants.

### ■ MATERIALS

Chart paper and colored markers, masking tape or pushpins.

### ■ PROCESS

1. Divide the large group into pairs of subgroups (each subgroup needs from one to five people).
2. Give each subgroup a sheet of chart paper and a colored marker. Tell the first subgroup in each pair to make a list of all of the conditions in any organization that maximize creativity, individuality, and trust. Tell the second subgroup in each pair to make a list of all of the conditions in any organization that could minimize trust and maximize dependency.
3. After about fifteen minutes, bring each pair of subgroups together and ask them to post their lists, side by side, on the wall.
4. Tell all members in each group to read over all of the items listed by both subgroups and then to underline only those statements that describe conditions that presently exist in their own organization. Each individual in each group should underline the conditions on all of the lists that have been made.
5. Discuss results.

From Interpersonal Conflict Resolution by Alan C. Filley. Copyright © 1975<br>Scott Foresman and Company. Reprinted by permission of the author.

**PROCESS NUMBER 6  REDUCING CONFLICT**

# GROUP CONVERSATION

### ■ DESCRIPTION

Group Conversation is a process that has been used in community groups to bring people together who traditionally have encountered barriers and roadblocks because of their differing ages, races, social status, ethnic backgrounds, religious backgrounds, economic levels, and educational levels.

### ■ APPLICATION

Use this process when a group needs to take time away from the task and focus on developing interpersonal relationships and connections. Conversations will focus on topics such as Red-Letter Days, Books I Have Loved, School Days, Family Holidays, What I Was Like as a Child, Rebellion, Then and Now, or Favorite Family Foods. This list is meant to be representative only.

### ■ TIME REQUIRED

One to two hours.

### ■ GROUP SIZE

Twenty to forty participants.

### ■ MATERIALS

None.

### ■ PROCESS

1. Meet with two or three key group members to select a topic for conversation. Be clear that this is a conversation and not a discussion. The difference is that individuals will be sharing about these topics at a personal level. The purpose of the conversation is to get to know each other as individuals—to share experiences, memories, backgrounds, life stories.
2. Develop a list of lead questions that will begin the conversation.
3. When the group has gathered together, sit in a circle where the leader can see the faces of all participants. If the group is larger than thirty, the leader may have to leave his or her chair once in awhile to accomplish this. Explain the goal of the Group Conversation.
   - Group Conversation is not group discussion such as we have when a problem is to be considered. Group Conversation is a way of matching our experiences around a topic of common interest. When one person is recounting his or her memories, the rest of us will find our own memories also bubbling over. Tell the group that you as leader will know by participants'

expressions or the wave of a hand that they want to be the next to speak.

4. Orient the group by asking a simple question (related to the topic) and asking each member to answer it going around in the circle. (For example, if the topic is, "What Were You Like as a Child?" then ask the question: Where were you when you were eight years old?) The leader answers first and then asks each group member to respond.

5. Set the stage by telling the group the questions around which the conversation will focus. Lead off by sharing your own answers to the questions.

6. Have someone chosen ahead of time who will act as co-leader to jump in and share if participants are slow to get started. Not everyone has to share. Some individuals will sit quietly and take in the conversation and emotions of others. Do not pressure people to share. The first question is the only one that requires everyone to answer.

7. The leader must function as a "weaver" throughout the conversation, holding questions in mind that can take the conversation in another direction or make connections between points that participants have made.

8. When the time is up, do not stop abruptly, but allow five to ten minutes for closing. In closing, look for the deeper significance of the topic to the group.

Adapted from *Reducing Social Tension and Conflict* by Rachel Davis DuBois and Mew-Soong Li, New York: Association Press, 1971.

## PROCESS NUMBER 7 REDUCING CONFLICT

# AIR TIME

### ■ DESCRIPTION

This process structures the amount of "air time" and makes sure that all participants have a share of the time available for discussion.

### ■ APPLICATION

Use one of the variations of this process when one or more group members monopolize the discussion, taking too much "air time."

### ■ TIME REQUIRED

Thirty to sixty minutes.

### ■ GROUP SIZE

Ten to thirty participants.

### ■ MATERIALS

None.

### ■ PROCESS

1. Variation One: Give each member the opportunity to state briefly in a round-robin

fashion his or her opinion or contribution. Members may opt to pass if they choose.

2. **Variation Two:** Divide the team into subgroups and have them record their ideas/suggestions on an overhead transparency or chart.

3. **Variation Three:** Distribute cards and ask each participant to write a comment or opinion on a card. Pass the cards to the leader, who shuffles them and deals them, one to each member. Each member then reads the comment or opinions on his or her card to the rest of the group.

Adapted from presentation by Dr. Wilma Smith on Site-Based Management,<br>Illinois Principals Association, St. Charles, Illinois, January 1990.

## PROCESS NUMBER  REDUCING CONFLICT

# WALKING A MILE IN THE OTHER'S MOCCASINS

### ■ DESCRIPTION
This process requires that opposing groups who are not listening to one another listen and then paraphrase the opposing point of view.

### ■ APPLICATION
Use this process when two groups are talking at each other, restating their points over and over again, and failing to listen to each other. This process can be used at any time in decision making or discussion at the discretion of the group leader.

### ■ TIME REQUIRED
Fifteen minutes.

### ■ GROUP SIZE
Fifteen to forty participants.

### ■ MATERIALS
Chart paper and magic markers, pushpins or masking tape.

### ■ PROCESS
1. Ask the group to stop talking. State the two points of view that you are hearing and write them on chart paper, chalkboard, or overhead.
2. Using the Fishbowl process, ask two representatives of each subgroup (A and B) to sit in the fishbowl. Have the chairs arranged so that the members face each other directly.
3. Have the representative from subgroup A state that group's point of view.
4. Have the representative from subgroup B paraphrase subgroup A's point of view to A's satisfaction.
5. Repeat the process for subgroup B.

Adapted from presentation by Dr. Wilma Smith on Site-Based Management,<br>Illinois Principals Association, St. Charles, Illinois, January 1990.

# CHAPTER NINE

# Group Processes for Goal Setting and Planning

**WHAT DOES A GOOD GOAL LOOK LIKE?**

**WHAT IS THE ESSENCE OF PLANNING?**

**WHAT PROCESS ACTIVITIES CAN HELP YOU SET APPROPRIATE GOALS AND PLAN EFFECTIVELY?**

## What does a good goal look like?

I've worked for bosses who never met a goal they didn't adopt. If at least one person suggested it during the goal-setting process, they were loathe to chop it from the final list. Accomplishing them all was something they rarely considered and apparently nobody checked. The process looked good on paper, but meant little to the troops in the trenches. The goal-setting process should not be an idle exercise that comes around annually, only to be greeted with the same enthusiasm that accompanies completing your income tax return. The goal-setting process should be welcomed as an opportunity to once again involve the participants in determining the major focus of the organization for a one-year, two-year, or five-year period.

> Far better it is to dare mighty things, to win glorious triumphs, even though checkered by failure, than to take rank with those poor spirits who neither enjoy much nor suffer much, because they live in the gray twilight that knows not victory or defeat.
> 
> —Teddy Roosevelt

> Plans identify events. People make them happen.
> 
> —Richard S. Sloma

If you want to make sure your goals get accomplished, here are the guidelines:

- Goals should be specific.
- Goals should be measurable.
- Goals should be results-centered.
- Goals should be realistic.
- Goals should be challenging.
- Goals should be flexible.
- Goals should be limited in number.[1]

> It is a critical requirement of effective leadership to redefine group roles and processes so that judgmental decisions are facilitated by judgmental techniques.
> —Delbecq, Van de Ven, and Gustafson

If the goals you and your team select meet all of these criteria, you will be well on your way to quality decision making.

## What is the essence of planning?

Once your cohesive, cooperative, and collegial team has identified problems, generated creative solutions, resolved conflicts, reached consensus about what to do, and defined the specific goals to be accomplished, there remains the work of planning. There are many teams who excel at plan development. But they have a difficult time delineating the activities and tasks, marshalling the resources that are essential, describing realistic time lines, and actually getting the job done. They have used all of their energies on the preliminary steps and now would like to walk away and let someone else actually do the backbreaking work.

> Planning is not a task or an event. Planning is first and foremost an attitude, a frame of mind.
> —Richard Sloma

The secret of successful planning is having the ability to start at the end point—the goal where you want to be—and work your way backward to where you are now. The skills of a chess master (the ability to see the end of the game and play it backward in the mind) are helpful to the master planner as well.

> No wind favors him who has no destined port.
> —Montaigne

## What process activities can help you set appropriate goals and plan effectively?

The following process activities are designed to help your team excel at goal setting and planning. They will take the drudgery and guesswork out of goal setting and planning and enable you to achieve positive results.

Each process will contain six parts: 1. Description, 2. Application, 3. Time Required, 4. Group Size, 5. Materials, and 6. Process.

> Planning means both to assess the future and make provision for it.
> — Henri Fayol

## PROCESS NUMBER 1 — GOAL SETTING AND PLANNING

# DELPHI PROCESS

### ■ DESCRIPTION

The Delphi Process was developed by the RAND Corporation to help make predictions about the future. It is a method of collecting opinions that help people make decisions. Participants respond to a series of questionnaires that are mailed or given to them. The questionnaires are returned, the results collated, and a second questionnaire is sent to the participants. On this questionnaire, the consensus of the group is reported and any participant whose answer lies outside the mean is asked to reconsider or justify his or her position. The original Delphi Process consisted of five rounds.

### ■ APPLICATION

The Delphi Process can be used for determining organizational goals, evaluating the effectiveness of current organizations or programs, and forecasting and planning for the future. It can also be used to poll people for their opinions on the choice of a strategy to implement a specific plan or to poll a large group about its preferences and priorities. This information can be used in the goal-setting process. The Delphi Process does not require a meeting, so it is useful when groups are scattered in various geographical locations. Since participants never meet face-to-face, everyone's anonymity is preserved.

### ■ TIME REQUIRED

At least one month.

### ■ GROUP SIZE

The Delphi Process has been used to gather information from six to three hundred individuals. A work group of from five to nine members to gather and process the information will be needed.

### ■ MATERIALS

Traditional Delphi Process: Multiple questionnaires developed by the work group for each participant. Modified Delphi Process: 3 × 5 cards for each participant.

## ■ PROCESS: TRADITIONAL DELPHI

1. Develop the Delphi Question.
2. Select and contact respondents.
3. Develop Questionnaire Number One.
4. Analyze Questionnaire Number One.
5. Develop Questionnaire Number Two.
6. Analyze Questionnaire Number Two.
7. Develop Questionnaire Number Three.
8. Analyze Questionnaire Number Three.
9. Prepare a final report.

Some Delphi Processes stop after two questionnaires. Some use cassette tapes for responses rather than questionnaires.

## ■ PROCESS: MODIFIED DELPHI

The following Modified Delphi Process can be used in a goal-setting process that involves multiple groups in a school district (parents, teachers, board members, classified personnel, administrators). Generate the responses and feedback when the groups are meeting to ensure participation.

1. Determine the specific question or problem to be considered by the group. The question or problem must be clearly stated so that each participant knows exactly what he or she is expected to answer (e.g., What goals do you believe this district should be working on next year?).
2. Fully explain the process from start to finish.
3. Using 3 × 5 cards, each participant will write his or her statements about the question or problem (one per card). The size of the group will determine how many cards each person will generate. The total number of cards that appears on the final printout should be no more than 100. If the group number is under twenty, then individuals can generate as many cards as they wish.
4. All individuals participating in the process should write their goals (ideas) using the same writing instrument so that no one card can be attributed to a certain individual.
5. When all participants have completed writing their statements, collect the cards. As cards are collected, they should be shuffled into the "deck." This will maintain the integrity and anonymity of the process.
6. When cards have been collected from all of the constituent groups, one or two individuals will cluster the responses. All of the cards in a cluster must be related and fit under the label given to that cluster.
7. All responses should then be typed under a label and, for clarity, each statement should be numbered consecutively throughout the clusters.

8. Each participant will then get two copies of the printout, one for establishing priorities to turn in, and one to keep to see how his or her ratings compare later with the group.
9. Each individual is asked to choose his or her top ten goals, top five goals, top two goals, and top goal.
10. Compute the results, arriving at a numerical total. Each of the top ten goals checked receives one point; items checked in the top five goals receive two points, items checked in the top two goals receive five points; an item checked as the top goal receives ten points. For each rating form, the scorer now totals the number of points attributed to an item from each participant. The item receiving the highest number of points becomes the number one priority, and so on through the top half dozen items. Fewer items than six are acceptable if a decided gap exists between any of the first few priorities. More than six goals might be adopted if a seventh or eighth rated goal was very close to six and seven in total points.
11. A list showing the totals is given to each participant and discussion is invited.

<small>The Delphi Process and Modified Delphi Process were adapted from *Odyssey to Excellence* by James Slezak, Millbrae, California: Merritt Publishing Co., 1984; and *Group Techniques for Program Planning: A Guide to Nominal Group and Delphi Processes* by Andre L. Delbecq, Andrew H. Van de Ven, and David H. Gustafson, Glenview, Illinois: Scott, Foresman and Company, 1975.</small>

## PROCESS NUMBER  2   GOAL SETTING AND PLANNING

# GROUP GOAL SETTING

### ■ DESCRIPTION
The Group Goal Setting process is a quick and easy method for a large group to consolidate many ideas into a few final goal statements.

### ■ APPLICATION
Use this process when time is limited, the group is small, and discussion and thought have preceded the actual process.

### ■ TIME REQUIRED
Thirty to forty-five minutes.

### ■ GROUP SIZE
Ten to twenty-five participants.

### ■ MATERIALS
Chart paper, masking tape or pushpins, strips of paper (18" × 4"), glue sticks for each group.

### ■ PROCESS
1. Post five or six pieces of chart paper around the room.

2. Ask participants to record their goals on strips of paper (one goal per strip).
3. Ask a participant to share one goal recorded on a strip of paper. Glue stick it to one sheet of chart paper.
4. Ask other participants to share strips that have the same or similar goals. Glue stick them to the same sheet of chart paper.
5. When all the goals that fit into the first category have been used, start another category.
6. Continue through the process until all strips of paper have been posted.
7. Go through each group of goals asking the group for general titles or categories.
8. Record each category over the stated goals and also on a separate sheet of memory paper, which will serve as the summary sheet.
9. Ask if there are any other categories that have been omitted. Individuals who had a goal that was not presented may add it to the list of goals.
10. Continue the process until all suggestions are exhausted.

Adapted from *Odyssey to Excellence* by James Slezak, San Francisco, California: Merritt Publishing Co., 1984.

## PROCESS NUMBER 3 — GOAL SETTING AND PLANNING
# NOMINAL GROUP TECHNIQUE

### ■ DESCRIPTION

The Nominal Group Technique has been described as silent brainstorming and was also included in Chapters Four and Six as a process for generating ideas. While Part One of the process is very similar to the formal brainstorming approach described earlier, Part Two of the process will assist teams in reducing the size of their list of items to a smaller list of items that will receive full evaluation.

### ■ APPLICATION

The Nominal Group Technique is a valuable process to use when confronting a problem that may have many answers. It is also helpful when teams are "stuck" on the same old solutions that don't seem to be working. This process also offers a quick and easy way to reduce the length of a list, giving every member an equal voice in the outcome. This approach will keep vocal team members from "running the show." If team members have been reluctant to share ideas in a public forum, the private nature of NGT will free them of inhibitions.

### ■ TIME REQUIRED

Sixty to ninety minutes.

## ■ GROUP SIZE
Five to thirty participants.

## ■ MATERIALS
3 × 5 cards and pencils for participants. Chart paper and colored markers for the recorders. Masking tape or pushpins to mount the chart paper.

## ■ PROCESS

### NOMINAL GROUP TECHNIQUE: PART ONE

1. Hang chart paper on walls prior to beginning of session. Provide enough chart paper to accommodate five or six ideas per sheet.
2. Clearly define the question or problem for the group. Writing the question or problem on chart paper, chalkboard, or overhead will help visual learners to remain focused.
3. Distribute two or three 3 × 5 cards to each participant (two cards if nine or more people, three cards if eight or fewer people).
4. Instruct participants to write one idea/solution/suggestion on each card. Use ten words or less. Print neatly. Allow five to ten minutes for this activity. (Another version of the NGT uses a round-robin recording of ideas similar to that used in formal brainstorming. Which method of "getting the ideas" you choose will depend on your group and its needs.)
5. Collect and shuffle cards for anonymity.
6. Ask for volunteers to write entries on chart paper (one person per sheet). Give all volunteers the same color marker (preferably dark—save the colored markers for part two).
   - No talking.
   - No more than six ideas per sheet, evenly spaced, with about six to eight inches between entries.
   - Do not number ideas.
   - Establish a six-inch left margin and draw a bullet on that margin at the beginning of each entry.
   - Absolutely no editing. Write each entry exactly as written on card, including spelling and/or syntax errors.
   - Be neat.
7. Ask volunteer recorders to return cards and markers to the facilitator.
8. Participants should read entries as they are being written on the sheets, searching for surprising ideas, and try to think of additional items that are inspired by what they are reading. Write any newly inspired ideas on a sheet of paper for later entry.

## NOMINAL GROUP TECHNIQUE: PART TWO

1. Take each idea in turn and make certain that there is agreement and understanding about what each item means and entails.
2. The team will now vote to reduce the initial list to a rank-ordered smaller list that they can discuss as a group. Each participant should rank order the five ideas/solutions that he or she feels are the most important. The most important idea receives a 5, the next a 4, and so on. Unranked items receive a zero.
3. Develop a chart to record the scores of each group member for his or her five most important ideas. Participants can give their rankings verbally to the chair who will record them on the chart.
4. In a larger group, you may prefer to use the following method of ranking. Give each participant five 3 × 5 cards (seven if the list is very long). Ask participants to select the five most important items and write them out in the center of each card, one item per card. They should then write the item's sequence number in the upper-left corner. While they are doing this, prepare a tally sheet to record the votes by writing as many numbers as there are items under consideration in the voting. Give participants a four-minute time limit for choosing and writing their five items. When everyone has completed this task, give the following instructions:
   - Spread the cards out in front of you so that you can see all five at once. Decide which card is more important than all the others. Write 5 in the lower-right-hand corner and underline it three times. Turn the card over.
   - Which is the least important of the four remaining cards? Write 1 in the lower-right-hand corner and underline it three times. Turn the card over.
   - Select the most important of the three remaining cards. Write 4 in the lower-right-corner and underline it three times. Turn the card over.
   - Select the least important of the two cards that are left. Write 2 in the lower-right corner and underline it three times.
   - Write 3 in the lower-right-hand corner of the last card and underline it three times.
5. Collect the cards. They may be shuffled to communicate to the participants that their voting will not be of concern to anyone.
6. Ask someone to assist you in reading off the votes or in recording the numbers. The reason the rankings are underlined is to keep you from confusing them with the item numbers.
7. Discuss the voting pattern.

8. Follow-up to the Nominal Group Technique will involve the interaction and discussion by group members regarding the highest ranked ideas/solutions and what action will be taken on the items.

Materials for the Nominal Group Technique were adapted from *Discussing and Deciding* by Scheidel and Crowell, New York: Macmillan Publishing Co., 1979; *Teaming for Quality Improvement* by H. D. Shuster, Englewood Cliffs, New Jersey: Prentice Hall, 1990; and *Group Techniques for Idea Building* by Carl M. Moore, Newbury Park, California: Sage Publications, 1987.

## PROCESS NUMBER 4 — GOAL SETTING AND PLANNING

# HOW?-BY PURSUIT

### ■ DESCRIPTION

The How?-By Pursuit is very similar to the Why?-Because Pursuit in its structure and use of a logic-pursuit diagram. The critical difference is that the How?-By Pursuit focuses on finding the steps that are needed to implement what is sometimes an abstract and very general recommendation.

### ■ APPLICATION

Use this process to develop a detailed plan of action. The object is not to recommend time lines and worry about resource acquisition, but to list all of the separate steps that will be needed to complete the plan.

### ■ TIME REQUIRED

One to two hours.

### ■ GROUP SIZE

Five to fifteen participants.

### ■ MATERIALS

Chart paper, colored markers, masking tape.

### ■ PROCESS

1. Tape a minimum of four pieces of chart paper together (horizontally, two by two) and tape them to the wall.
2. Write the solution/recommendation/goal statement at the left center and enclose it in a box.
3. Write the word "How?" above the box.
4. Draw the first vertical line of the logic tree.
5. Seek specific ways to implement the boxed statement/recommendation.
6. The answer to the question "How?" will be the statement "By" followed by a verb.
7. Continue maintaining logical linkages horizontally.
8. When collapsing the logic tree, do not combine horizontally, collapse vertically.

Adapted from *Teaming for Quality Improvement* by H. David Shuster, Englewood Cliffs, New Jersey: Prentice Hall, 1990. Used by permission of author.

# HOW?–BY PURSUIT DIAGRAM

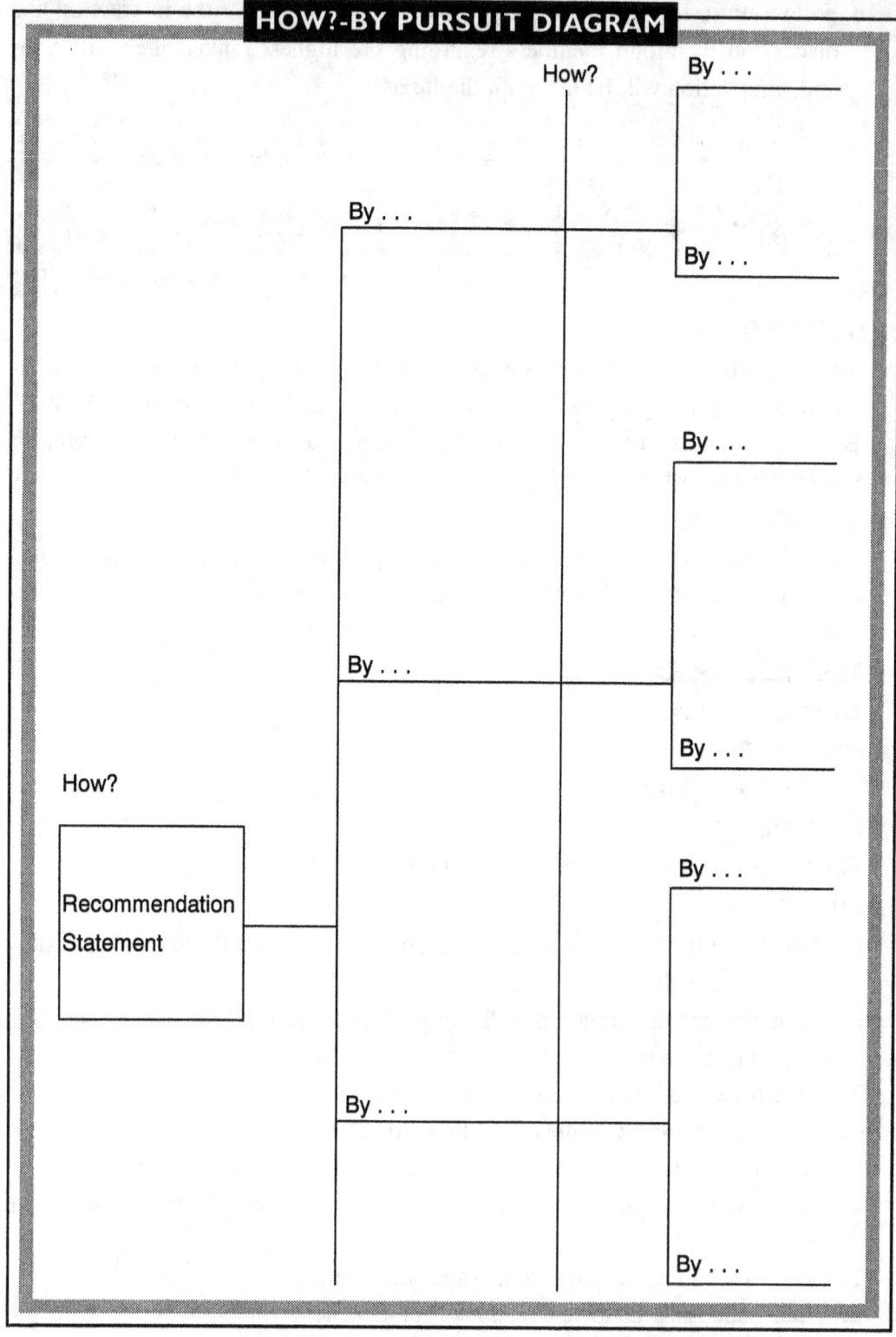

Adapted from *Teaming for Quality Improvement* by H. David Shuster, Englewood Cliffs, New Jersey: Prentice Hall, 1990. Used by permission of author.

# PROCESS NUMBER 5 — GOAL SETTING AND PLANNING

## MODIFIED MAPS

### ■ DESCRIPTION
The MAPS (Map Action Planning System) was originally developed at McGill University by Marsha Forest and Evelyn Lusthaus and was intended as a planning process for students with disabilities. It has been adapted here for use in a group planning process and is essentially a list-making exercise that responds to six key questions. The process can be used to elicit important information that is relevant to the development of a plan or proposal.

### ■ APPLICATION
The Modified MAPS process is a creative variation to use for global team planning.

### ■ TIME REQUIRED
Thirty to forty-five minutes.

### ■ GROUP SIZE
Six to twelve participants.

### ■ MATERIALS
Chart paper, colored markers, pushpins or masking tape.

### ■ PROCESS
1. On a large piece of chart paper draw the MAP Questions (see diagram).
2. The group chair or facilitator goes through each of the six key questions. A recorder lists the group's responses.
   - What is the story or history of our group? organization? school?
   - What is our dream? our vision?
   - What is our worst nightmare?
   - Who are we? What are the key participants like as individuals?
   - What are our gifts, strengths, talents?
   - What are our needs?
3. Using the information collected, the group will develop an action plan.

Adapted from the MAPS Action Planning System in the article "Everyone Belongs" by Marsha Forest and Evelyn Lusthaus. *Teaching Exceptional Children*, Winter, 1990, v. 22, n.2, pp. 32–35.

## THE MAP QUESTIONS

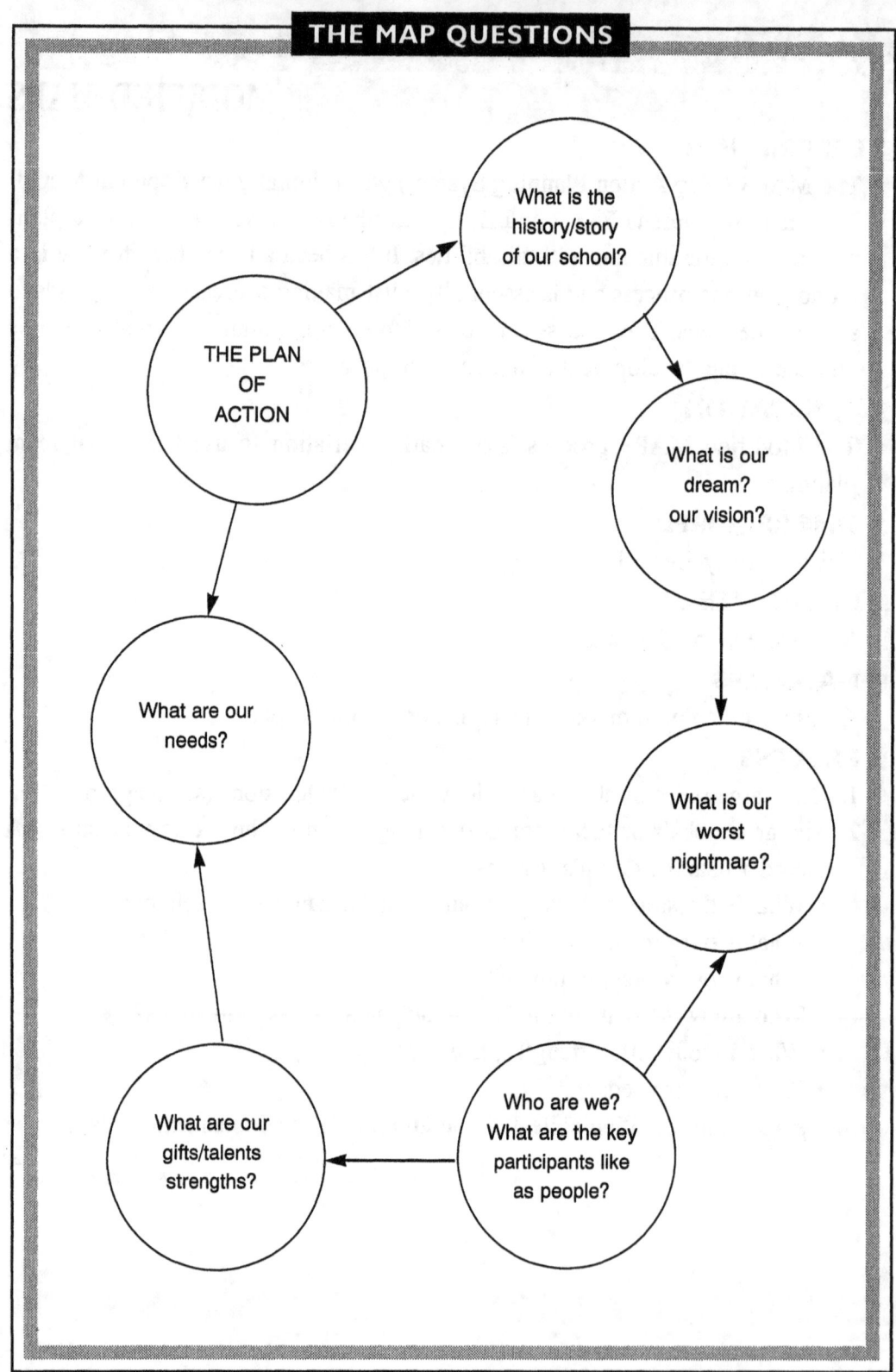

## SAMPLE MAP

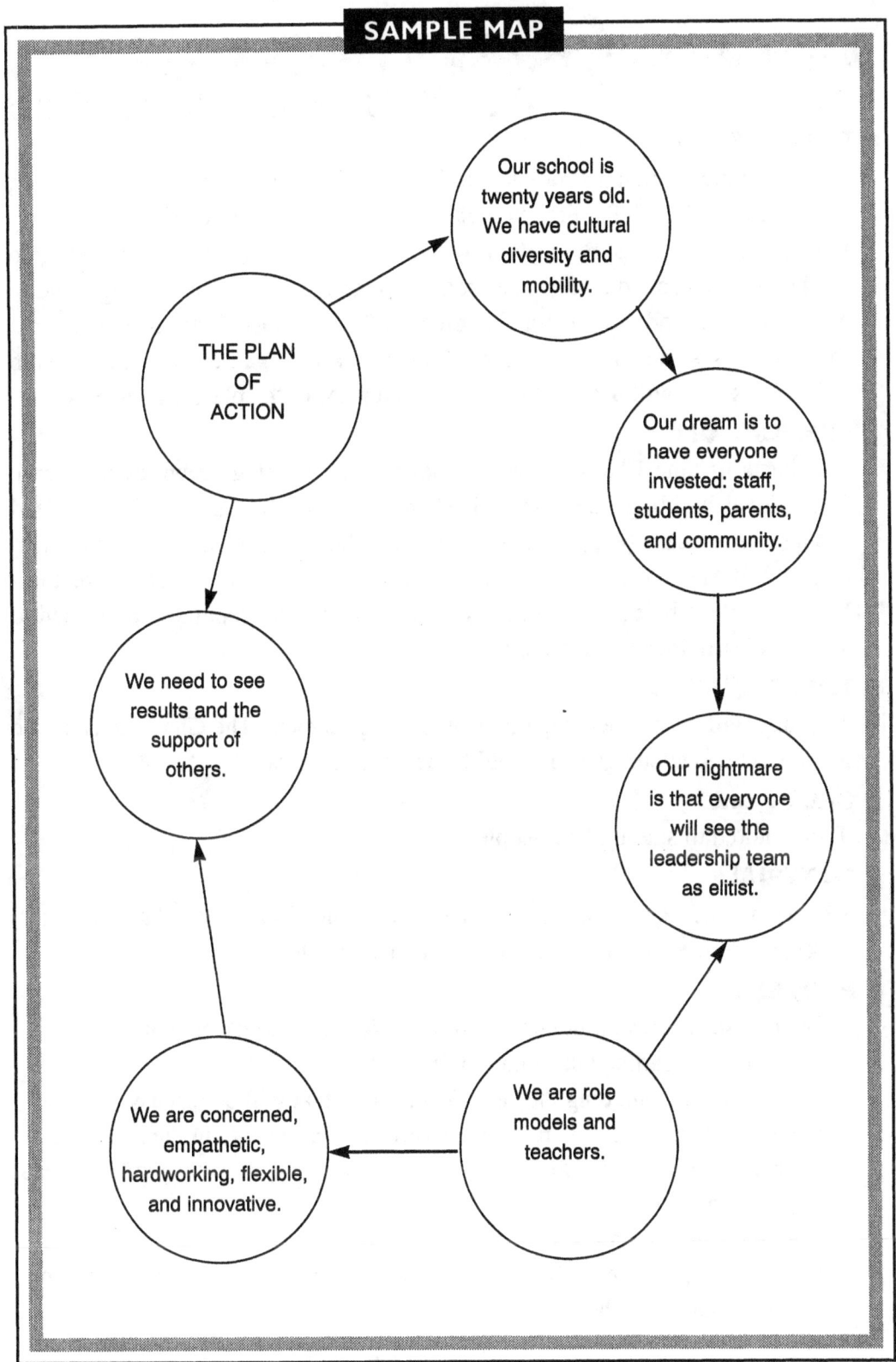

165

## PROCESS NUMBER 6 — GOAL SETTING AND PLANNING

# CHARRETTE PLANNING PROCESS

### ■ DESCRIPTION

The Charrette Planning Process gets its name from the French word meaning small cart. In the 1800s, French architectural students used these carts to carry their exercises to class. Students who had not completed their work would jump on the cart as it rolled along. The process consists of intensive meetings held in a condensed period of time with subgroups of individuals. There is often a large total group session as well. The sessions are used to gather information from individuals who will have a stake in the plan prior to the planning process.

### ■ APPLICATION

Architects use the Charrette prior to developing working drawings of a large institutional building like a school when input from a variety of specialized groups is necessary (e.g., librarians, early childhood teachers, classroom teachers, etc.). It can be used whenever a large-scale plan that will affect a large number of people is being developed and when experts and resources are needed to assist the participants in the process.

### ■ TIME REQUIRED

The time will vary depending on what is being planned. The Charrette could be as short as two evenings or it could be as long as one week.

### ■ GROUP SIZE

Two hundred to six hundred people.

### ■ MATERIALS

All materials that will be shared with participants (charts, graphs, overheads, slides, models, etc.) should be prepared and available.

### ■ PROCESS

1. Select a steering committee to plan the series of Charrette meetings.
   - Identify all participants who will be involved.
   - Collect data regarding the significant issues that will be discussed.
   - Select appropriate experts and authorities to participate in the meetings.
   - Prepare necessary materials for the meetings (overheads, slides, drawings, models).
2. Hold the Charrette meetings.
3. Hold a large public meeting to present conclusions after all of the small group meetings have been held.

Process adapted from *Groups: Theory and Experience* by Rodney W. Napier and Matti K. Gershenfeld, Boston: Houghton Mifflin, 1981; and *Discussing and Deciding* by Scheidel and Crowell, New York: Macmillan Publishing Co., 1979.

**PROCESS NUMBER 7  GOAL SETTING AND PLANNING**

# MIXED SCANNING STRATEGY

## ■ DESCRIPTION

The Mixed Scanning Strategy to be used in the planning process enables the participants to build in checkpoints along the way that allow for changing or dropping the plan without major fallout.

## ■ APPLICATION

Use this strategy when you are implementing a very complex, expensive, and risky plan.

## ■ TIME REQUIRED

The strategy will be applied at stages during the implementation.

## ■ GROUP SIZE

Any size.

## ■ MATERIALS

Chart paper, colored markers, pushpins or masking tape.

## ■ PROCESS

1. When possible, **fragment the implementation** into several serial steps. It will be easier to monitor and evaluate the progress of implementation when it can be viewed in smaller steps rather than as one total act.

2. When possible, **divide the commitment to implement** into several serial steps. This is a political rule. If persons must give full and complete commitment to a proposed project before it is even started, there may be greater hesitation about beginning. It therefore may be useful to require only partial commitment prior to instituting a program with increasing support required in successive stages.

3. When possible, **divide the commitment of assets into several serial steps** and maintain a strategic reserve. This is simply the old rule that we should not put all our eggs into one basket.

4. If possible, arrange implementation so that **costly and less reversible decisions will appear later in the process** than those that are more reversible and less costly. Again, this step is calculated to prevent waste if the plan fails or is dropped along the line as it is being put into action.

5. Provide a **time schedule for additional collection and processing of information** so that information will be available at key turning points between steps of the implementation schedule. This is to have the needed information

available so group members can assess whether to move from one step to the next, whether to modify the steps of implementation, or whether to abandon the program.

Reprinted with permission of authors from Scheidel, Thomas M., and Crowell, Laura, *Discussing and Deciding: A Desk Book for Group Leaders and Members.* New York: Macmillan. Copyright © 1979.

## PROCESS NUMBER  GOAL SETTING AND PLANNING

# FLOWCHARTS

### ■ DESCRIPTION

Flowcharts are a means of portraying in graphic form the sequence of events in a process or plan. They are constructed of boxes or outlines of various shapes with connecting arrows and flow lines.

### ■ APPLICATION

Use a flowchart when the plan is unusually complex or when a large number of people will benefit from having the plan visually displayed. Some teams find it useful to display a flowchart of their yearly goals where everyone can have a sense of what is happening and when.

### ■ TIME REQUIRED

Forty-five to ninety minutes.

### ■ GROUP SIZE

Seven to fifteen audience members.

### ■ MATERIALS

Butcher paper, colored markers, masking tape.

### ■ PROCESS

There is a "flowchart language" that is used in business wherein certain shapes designate certain operations. You may choose to develop your own flowchart shorthand, but the symbols are provided for your information.

- The start or end of the flowchart is a horizontal oval. All plans have a beginning and an end. Only two of these outlines are used in any one process, one at the beginning and one at the end.
- The input or output outline is a parallelogram; the vertical lines are angled to give the illusion of movement. Written documents like memos, reports, notes, would appear inside a parallelogram.
- Any transformation, movement, step, or process in the plan will appear inside the process outline, which is a rectangle.

- Any situation that depicts an activity requiring a choice will appear in the decision outline, which is diamond shaped with alternative paths clearly marked. ◇
- The connectors are circles used to show entering or leaving the process. Typically, connectors are labeled with letters to indicate where to leave off and where to pick up. They can indicate that the remainder of the flowchart can be found on another page or sheet. ○

1. Write your starting point in a horizontal oval at the left of a large piece of butcher paper. Tear off enough so that you will not have to "paste" your flow-chart in too many places.
2. It may be helpful to write a brief description of the steps to assist you as you build the flowchart.
3. Modifications to earlier parts of the chart may be made as you progress.
4. Once the chart has been completed, reproduce it in a smaller format with all of the corrections and additions included.
5. Post the butcher paper flowchart as is, or redraw a totally accurate one for posting in a central location.

Adapted from *Teamwork: Involving People in Quality and Productivity Improvement* by Charles A. Aubrey, II and Patricia K. Felkins, Milwaukee, Wisconsin: American Society for Quality Control, 1988.

PROCESS NUMBER 9   GOAL SETTING AND PLANNING

# ACTION LOGS

## ■ DESCRIPTION

Action Logs are simply charts or spreadsheets of the basic activities required to complete a particular goal. They identify the goals that must be met, list the activities required to accomplish each goal, the names of the individuals who are responsible, a date by which the activity must be accomplished, and a date when the activity was actually accomplished.

## ■ APPLICATION

Use this simple chart whenever you have a goal to accomplish.

## ■ TIME REQUIRED

Thirty to sixty minutes depending on the complexity of the goal and the number of activities needed to accomplish the goal.

## ■ GROUP SIZE

Not applicable.

## ■ MATERIALS

The chart can be hand drawn or developed from a database spreadsheet.

## ■ PROCESS

1. Write the goal across the top of the Action Log.
2. Develop columns for the following headings: Activity, Person(s) Responsible, Resources Needed, Date to Be Completed, Date Completed.
3. Complete all information.
4. Enter dates completed as activities are crossed off your "to do" list.

Adapted from *Teamwork: Involving People in Quality and Productivity Improvement* by Charles A. Aubrey, II and Patricia K. Felkins, Milwaukee, Wisconsin: American Society for Quality Control, 1988.

### SAMPLE ACTION LOG

**DISTRICT GOAL: DEVELOP A TECHNOLOGY PLAN**

| Activity | By Whom | By When | Resources | Completed |
|---|---|---|---|---|
| Send out opportunity-to-serve notices to all staff. | Asst. Supt | Sept. 1 | | |
| Select representatives for the following subcommittees: Middle School Technology Center, Instructional Technology, Library Automation, Administrative Technology, Long-Distance Learning, and Staff Development. | Ad. Council | Sept. 15 | | |
| Convene all representatives for large group meeting to discuss goals, timelines, and parameters; appoint chairpersons. | Asst. Supt. | Oct. 1 | | |
| Convene each subcommittee to write committee missions. | Chairpersons | November 1 | | |
| Convene consultants/experts to share state of art in each area. | Consultants and Chairpersons | December-January | | |
| Convene Technology Committee to hear reports from each subcommittee. | Asst. Supt. | February | | |
| Draft recommendations. | Committee | February | | |
| Send to writing committee for editing/revisions. | Writing Committee | March | | |
| Convene Technology Comm. for final approval of plan. | Technology Committee | March | | |
| Present plan to Ad. Council. | Asst. Supt. | April | | |
| Present plan to Faculty Advisory | Asst. Supt. Committee Members | April | | |
| Present plan to Citizens Group | Asst. Supt. | April | | |

# PROCESS NUMBER 10 — GOAL SETTING AND PLANNING

# THE PATH

## ■ DESCRIPTION

The PATH is a visionary process that can be used to formulate a one- (or more) year plan. The process utilizes six questions that, when answered, can help a group determine where they need to focus their energies.

## ■ APPLICATION

This process can be used with groups who may be goal setting together for the first time (e.g., board of education committee, community group, local school council). The questions allow ample opportunity to discussion and help to "tease out" the critical values and issues of the group mission or vision statement.

## ■ TIME REQUIRED

One and one-half to two hours.

## ■ GROUP SIZE

Five to fifteen participants.

## ■ MATERIALS

Chart paper and colored markers, pushpins or masking tape.

## ■ PROCESS

1. Give each participant a copy of the PATH Process Diagram.
2. Post a copy of the PATH Process Diagram that will be completed as the group discusses each question.

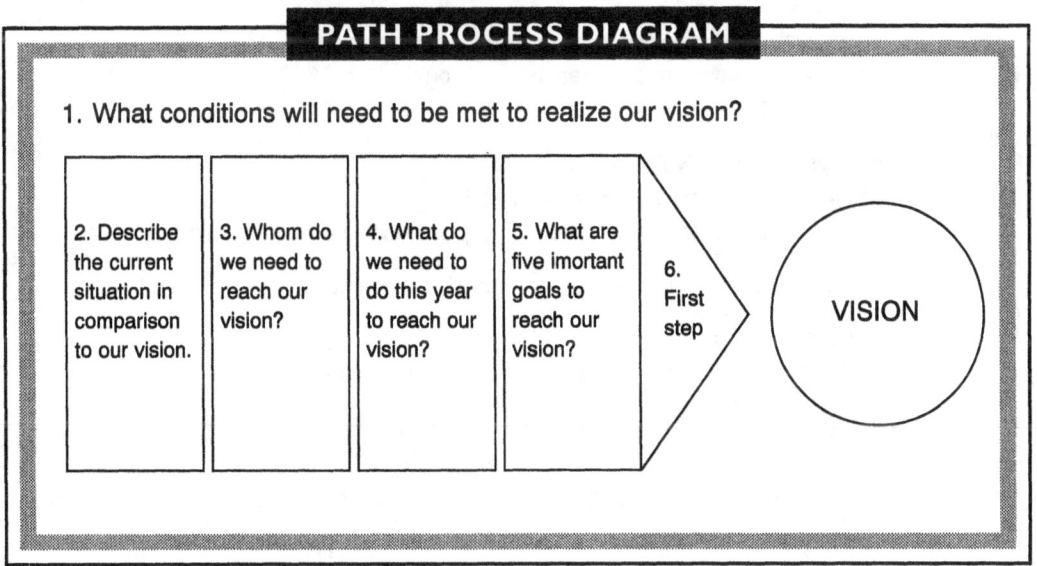

3. Determine what vision statement will be used for Question Number One (e.g., What conditions will need to be met for our district to be considered an excellent school district?).
4. Briefly discuss each question, placing reasons in the appropriate spaces.
5. Determine whether additional processes are needed to select the goals to be targeted.

---

**PATH PROCESS SAMPLE**

1. What conditions will need to be met to realize our vision?

| 2. Describe the current situation in comparison to our vision. | 3. Whom do we need to reach our vision? | 4. What do we need to do this year to reach our vision? | 5. What are five imortant goals to reach our vision? | 6. First step | VISION |

The Process was completed by a board of education finance committee.

Question #1: What will we need for our district to be considered an excellent school district?
- Complete middle school program
- Addition built to the current junior high school
- A successful referendum
- Several academic programs restored that had been cut

Question #2: Describe the school district now in comparison to our vision.
- Short on space
- Programs cut
- In debt
- Class sizes increasing

Question #3: Whom do we need to reach our vision?
- Community
- Staff
- Legislators to solve funding problems

Question #4.: What do we need to do this year?
- Committees to work on middle school plan (visits, schedules, teams)
- Plan a fall referendum
- Share discussion with whole board and get their support
- Keep community informed
- Invite legislators to meeting

Question #5: What are three important steps to reach our vision?
- Pass referendum
- Gain community support for middle school concept
- Lobby for increase funding for education in district

---

[1] C. A. Aubrey, II and P. K. Felkins. *Teamwork*, (Milwaukee, Wisconsin: ASQC Quality Press, 1988), 94.

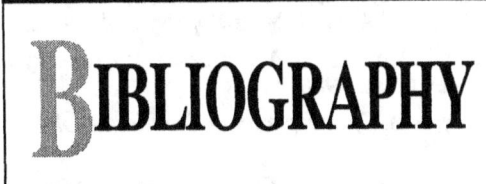

# BIBLIOGRAPHY

Adams, James L. *Conceptual Blockbusting: A Guide to Better Ideas.* Reading, Massachusetts: Addison-Wesley Publishing Company, 1986.

Allen, Lew, and Carl D. Glickman. "School Improvement: The Elusive Faces of Shared Governance," *NASSP Bulletin* 76, no. 54 (March 1992): 80–87.

Ambrose, Frank. "The Case for Collaborative, Versus Negotiated, Decision Making," *NASSP Bulletin* 73, no. 518 (Sept. 1989): 56–59.

Argyris, Chris. *Intervention Theory and Method: A Behavioral Science View.* Reading, Massachusetts: Addison-Wesley Publishing Company, 1970.

Arhar, Joanne M., J. Howard Johnston, and Glenn C. Markle. "The Effects of Teaming and Other Collaborative Arrangements." *Middle School Journal* 19, no. 3 (May 1988): 28–32.

Ashton, Patricia T., and Rodman B. Webb. *Making a Difference: Teachers' Sense of Efficacy and Student Achievement.* New York: Longman, 1986.

Aubrey, Charles A., II, and Patricia K. Felkins. *Teamwork: Involving People in Quality and Productivity Improvement.* Milwaukee, Wisconsin: American Society for Quality Control, 1988.

Auvine, Brian, Betsy Densmore, Mary Extrom, Scott Poole, and Michel Shanklin. *A Manual for Group Facilitators.* Madison, Wisconsin: The Center for Conflict Resolution, 1985.

Bavelas, Alex. "Communication Patterns in Task-Oriented Groups," *Journal of the Acoustical Society of America,* Vol. 22 (1950): 725-730.

Beal, George M., Joe M. Bohlen, and J. Neil Raudabaugh. *Leadership and Dynamic Group Action.* Ames, Iowa: The Iowa State University Press, 1962.

Brightman, Harvey J. "Improving Principals' Performance Through Training in the Decision Sciences," *Educational Leadership* 41, no. 5 (February 1984): 50–56.

Carroll, John S., and Eric J. Johnson. "Decision Research: A Field Guide." *Applied Social Research Methods Series,* Volume 22. Newbury Park, California: Sage Publications, 1990.

Chamley, John D., Fred R. McFarlane, Russell L. Young, and Ellen M. Caprio. "Overcoming the Superprincipal Complex: Shared and Informed Decision Making." *NASSP Bulletin* 76, no. 540 (January 1992): 1–8.

Conley, Sharon C. "Who's on First? School Reform, Teacher Participation, and the Decision-Making Process." *Education and Urban Society* 21, no. 4 (August 1989): 366–379.

Conway, James A. "The Myth, Mystery, and Mastery of Participative Decision Making in Education." *Educational Administration Quarterly* 20, no. 3 (Summer 1984): 11–40.

deBono, Edward. *Lateral Thinking: Creativity Step by Step.* New York: Harper & Row Publishers, 1970.

Delbecq, Andre L., Andrew H. Van de Ven, and David H. Gustafson. *Group Techniques for Program Planning: A Guide to Nominal Group and Delphi Processes.* Glenview, Illinois: Scott, Foresman and Company, 1975.

Doyle, Michael, and David Straus. *How to Make Meetings Work.* New York: The Berkley Publishing Group, 1986.

DuBois, Rachel Davis, and Mew-Soong Li. *Reducing Social Tension and Conflict.* New York: Association Press, 1971.

Duttweiler, Patricia Cloud. "Recommendations for Implementing School-Based Management/Shared Decision Making." *Insights on Educatonal Policy and Practice,* ED no. 33 0061. no. 21, (July 1990).

Dyer, William G. *Team Building: Issues and Alternatives.* Reading, Massachusetts: Addison-Wesley Publishing Company, 1977.

Einhorn, Hillel J., and Robin M. Hogarth. "Behavioral Decision Theory: Processes of Judgment and Choice." *Annual Review of Psychology* 32: 1981: 53–88.

Etzioni, Amitai. *The Active Society: A Theory of Societal and Political Processes,* New York: The Free Press, 1986.

Filley, Alan C. *Interpersonal Conflict Resolution.* Glenview, Illinois: Scott, Foresman and Company, 1975.

Forest, Marsha, and Evelyn Lusthaus. "Everyone Belongs." *Teaching Exceptional Children* 22, 1990: 32–35.

Francis, Dave, and Don Young. *Improving Work Groups: A Practical Manual for Team Building.* La Jolla, California: University Associates, 1979.

Gordon, Thomas. *Leader Effectiveness Training.* New York: G. P. Putnam's Sons, 1977.

Guthrie, Ellen, and Warren Sam Miller. *Process Politics: A Guide for Group Leaders.* San Diego, California: University Associates, 1981.

Guzzo, Richard A., Ed. *Improving Group Decision Making in Organizations: Approaches from Theory and Research.* New York: Academic Press, 1982.

Hale, Norman, and John Lindelow. "Solving Problems." In *School Leadership: Handbook for Survival,* edited by Stuart C. Smith, Jo Ann Mazzarella, and Philip K. Piele. Eugene, Oregon: Clearinghouse on Educational Management, 1981.

Hansen, Barbara J., and Carl L. Marburger. *School-Based Improvement: A Manual for Training School Councils.* Columbia, Maryland: National Committee for Citizens in Education, 1989.

Hare, A. Paul. *Handbook of Small Group Research,* 2nd ed. New York: The Free Press, 1976.

Huddleston, Judith, Margaret Claspell, and Joellen Killion. "Participative Decision Making Can Capitalize on Teacher Expertise. *NASSP Bulletin* 75, no. 534 (April 1991): 80–89.

Hyman, Ronald T. *School Administrator's Staff Development Activities Manual.* Englewood Cliffs, New Jersey: Prentice Hall, Inc., 1986.

Janis, Irving L. "Groupthink." In *Readings in Managerial Psychology,* edited by Harold J. Leavitt, Louis R. Pondy, and David M. Boje. Chicago: University of Chicago Press, 1980.

Janis, Irving L., and Leon Mann. *Decision-Making: A Psychological Analysis of Conflict, Choice, and Commitment.* New York: The Free Press, 1977.

Johnson, David W., and Frank P. Johnson. *Joining Together: Group Theory and Group Skills.* Englewood Cliffs, New Jersey: Prentice Hall, Inc., 1982.

Johnson, David W., and Roger T. Johnson. *Leading the Cooperative School.* Edina, Minnesota: Interaction Book Company, 1989.

Joyce, Bruce, James Wolf, and Emily Calhoun. *The Self-Renewing School.* Alexandria, Virginia: Association for Supervision and Curriculum Development, 1993.

Kepner, Charles H., and Benjamin Tregoe. *The Rational Manager.* New York: McGraw-Hill Book Company, 1965.

Kirby, Peggy C. "Shared Decision Making: Moving from Concerns about Restrooms to Concerns about Classrooms." *Journal of School Leadership* 2, (July 1992): 330–344.

Koehn, John J. "Dealing with Hidden Agendas: Try 'Parking Lot Meetings'," *The Developer,* No. 3, (February 1994) 3-4.

Lee, Irving J. "Procedures for Coercing Agreements," *Harvard Business Review,* 32 (January-February 1954): 39-45.

Likert, Rensis. *New Patterns of Management.* New York: McGraw-Hill Book Company, 1961.

Lynch, Robert F., and Thomas J. Werner. *Continuous Improvement: Teams and Tools.* Atlanta, Georgia: QualTeam, 1992.

McGregor, Douglas. *The Human Side of Enterprise.* New York: McGraw-Hill Book Company, 1960.

Mill, Cyril R. *Activities for Trainers: 50 Useful Designs.* San Diego, California: University Associates, 1980.

Moore, Carl M. *Group Techniques for Idea Building.* Newbury Park, California: Sage Publications, 1987.

Mutchler, Sue E. "Shared Decision Making: Harnessing the Energy of People." *Insights on Educational Policy and Practice,* no. 16 (December 1989).

Napier, Rodney, and Matti K. Gershenfeld. *Groups: Theory and Experience,* 2nd ed. Boston: Houghton Mifflin, 1981.

Nutt, Paul C. *Making Tough Decisions: Tactics for Improving Managerial Decision Making.* San Francisco: Jossey-Bass, 1989.

Osborn, Alex F. *Applied Imagination: Principles and Procedures of Creative Problem Solving.* New York: Charles Scribner & Sons, 1963.

Parish, Ralph, Eugene Eubanks, Frank D. Aquila, and Sandra Walker, "Knock at Any School," *Phi Delta Kappan* 70, no. 5, 393–394.

Parker, Glenn M. *Team Players and Teamwork.* San Francisco: Jossey-Bass Publishers, 1990.

Parnes, Sidney. *The Magic of Your Mind.* Buffalo, New York: Creative Education Foundation, 1981.

Pfeiffer, J. William, Ed. *A Handbook of Structured Experiences for Human Relations Training* Volume IX. San Diego, California: University Associates, 1983.

Prince, George M. *The Practice of Creativity: A Manual for Dynamic Group Problem Solving.* New York: Harper & Row Publishers, 1970.

Robson, Mike. *Quality Circles in Action.* Brookfield, Vermont: Gower Publishing Company, 1984.

Roy, Patricia A., and Patrick O'Brien. "Together We Can Make It Better in Collaborative Schools." *Journal of Staff Development* 12, no. 3 (Summer 1991), 47–51.

Russell, John J., Bruce S. Cooper, and Ruth B. Greenblatt. "How Do You Measure Shared Decision Making?" *Educational Leadership* 50, no. 1, (September 1992): 39–40.

Saphier, Jon, and Matthew King. "Good Seeds Grow in Strong Cultures." *Educational Leadership* 42, no. 6 (March 1985), 67–74.

Scheidel, Thomas M., and Laura Crowell. *Discussing and Deciding: A Desk Book for Group Leaders and Members.* New York: Macmillan Publishing Co., Inc., 1979.

Schein, Edgar H. "Coming to a New Awareness of Organizational Culture." *Sloan Management Review* 25 (1969): 3–16.

Schmuck, Richard A., Philip J. Runkel, Jane H. Arends, and Richard I. Arends. *The Second Handbook of Organization Development in Schools.* Eugene, Oregon: Center for Educational Policy and Management. Mayfield, Colorado: Palo Alto Publishers, 1977.

Shuster, H. David. *Teaming for Quality Improvement: A Process for Innovation and Consensus.* Englewood Cliffs, New Jersey: Prentice Hall, Inc., 1990.

Slezak, James. *Odyssey to Excellence.* San Franciso, California: Merritt Publishing Company, 1984.

Sloma, Richard S. *No-Nonsense Planning.* New York: The Free Press, 1984.

Villa, Richard A., Jacqueline S. Thousand, William Stainback, and Susan Stainback. *Restructuring for Caring and Effective Education: An Administrative Guide to Creating Heterogeneous Schools.* Baltimore: Paul H. Brookes Publishing Co., 1992.

von Oech, Roger. *A Whack on the Side of the Head.* New York: Warner Books, 1983.

Wellins, Richard S., William S. Byham, and Jeanne M. Wilson. *Empowered Teams.* San Francisco: Jossey-Bass Publishers, 1991.

Wheeler, Daniel D., and Irving L. Janis. *A Practical Guide for Making Decisions.* New York: The Free Press, 1980.

Wood, Carolyn. "Participatory Decision Making: Why Doesn't It Seem to Work?" *The Educational Forum* 49, no. 1, (Fall 1984): 55–64.

Zumwalt, Karen K., Ed. *Improving Teaching.* Alexandria, Virginia: ASCD, 1986.

# QUOTATION CITATIONS

## ■ CHAPTER ONE

1. Robert Townsend. *Up the Organization: How to Stop the Corporation from Stifling People and Strangling Profits.* New York: Alfred A. Knopf, 1981, 45.
2. Virginia Simon quoted in Irving L. Janis and Leon Mann. *Decision Making: A Psychological Analysis of Conflict, Choice, and Commitment.* New York: The Free Press, 1977, 5.
3. Casey Stengel.
4. Fred Allen.
5. Milton Berle.
6. Ecclesiastes 4:9–13 *The Living Bible.* Wheaton, Illinois: Tyndale House Publishers, 1971.
7. Olaf Helmer. *Omni* pp. 81–90. May, 1981, 81.
8. John S. Carroll and Eric J. Johnson. "Decision Research: A Field Guide." *Applied Social Research Methods Series,* Volume 22. Newbury Park, California: SAGE Publications, 1990, 19.
9. Daniel D. Wheeler and Irving L. Janis. *A Practical Guide for Making Decisions.* New York: The Free Press, 1980, 5.
10. Anonymous.

## ■ CHAPTER TWO

1. Robert F. Lynch and Thomas J. Werner. *Continuous Improvement: Teams and Tools.* Atlanta, Georgia: QualTeam, Inc., 1992, 44.
2. Jon Saphier and Matthew King. "Good Seeds Grow in Strong Cultures," *Educational Leadership,* March 1985, 87.

## ■ CHAPTER THREE

1. Glenn M. Parker. *Team Players and Teamwork.* San Francisco: Jossey-Bass Publishers, 1990, 16.
2. Dave Francis and Don Young. *Improving Work Groups: A Practical Manual for Team Buiding.* La Jolla, California: University Associates, 1979, 8.
3. Robert F. Lynch and Thomas J. Werner. *Continuous Improvement: Teams and Tools.* Atlanta, Georgia: QualTeam, Inc., 1992, 7.

## ■ CHAPTER FOUR

1. Edward deBono. *Lateral Thinking: Creativity Step by Step.* New York: Harper & Row Publishers, 1970, 11.
2. Albert Szent-Gyorgyi, quoted in Roger von Oech. *A Whack on the Side of the Head: How to Unlock Your Mind for Innovation.* New York: Warner Books, 1983, 7.
3. Albert Einstein quoted in Eugene Raudsepp. "Can You Trust Your Hunches?" *Management Review,* Volume XLIX, no. 4 (a), April 1960, 7.

■ CHAPTER FIVE

1. Benjamin Franklin.
2. Thomas M. Scheidel and Laura Crowell. *Discussing and Deciding: A Desk Book for Group Leaders and Members.* New York: Macmillan Publishing Co., Inc., 1979, 17.
3. Charles H. Kepner and Benjamin B. Tregoe. *The Rational Manager: A Systematic Approach to Problem Solving and Decision Making.* New York: McGraw-Hill Book Company, 1965, 39.

■ CHAPTER SIX

1. Albert Einstein.
2. H. L. Mencken.
3. Charlie Brown.
4. Robert F. Lynch and Thomas J. Werner. *Continuous Improvement: Teams and Tools.* Atlanta, Georgia: QualTeam, Inc., 1992, 159.

■ CHAPTER SEVEN

1. David W. Johnson and Frank P. Johnson. *Joining Together: Group Theory and Group Skills.* Englewood Cliffs, New Jersey: Prentice Hall, Inc. 1982, 107.
2. Robert F. Lynch and Thomas J. Werner. *Continuous Improvement: Teams and Tools.* Atlanta, Georgia: QualTeam, Inc., 1992, 226.

■ CHAPTER EIGHT

1. Walt Whitman.
2. Alan C. Filley. *Interpersonal Conflict Resolution,* Glenview, Illinois: Scott, Foresman and Company, 1975, 1.
3. Rachel David DuBois and Mew-Soong Li. *Reducing Social Tension and Conflict.* New York: Association Press, 1971, 49.

■ CHAPTER NINE

1. Montaigne.
2. Teddy Roosevelt.
3. Richard S. Sloma, *No-Nonsense Planning.* New York: The Free Press, 1984, 41.
4. Ibid.
5. Andre L. Delbecq, Andrew H. Van de Ven and David H. Gustafson. *Group Techniques for Program Planning: A Guide to Nominal Group and Delphi Processes.* Glenview, Illinois: Scott Foresman and Company, 1975, 6.
6. Henri Fayol. *General and Industrial Management,* trans. Constance Storrs. London: Pitman, 1949, 43.

# INDEX

Achieving Consensus, process activities for, 117–138
    Advocacy Subgroups, 125–126
    Apollo Process, 117–118
        modified, 119–120
    Consensus Brainstorming, 125
    Diamonds Nine, 129
    Fist-to-Five, 133–134
    Huddle Method, The, 122
    Multivoting, 131
    Parking Lot Meetings, 128
    Priority Matrix, 135–138
    Ranking, 127–128
    Scanning Strategy, 132
    Spend-a-Buck, 134–135
    Vigilant Analysis, 123
Action Logs, 169–170
    sample, 170
Adams, James, 69
Advocacy Subgroups, 125–126
Affinity Process, 103–104
    diagram, 104
Air Time, 151–152
Allen, Fred, 11
Apollo Process, 117–118
    modified, 119–120
    sample, 120
Are We Really a Team?, 56–59
    checklist, 57–59

Berle, Milton, 5
Brainstorming, 68–72
Broken Squares, 38–41
    Participant Instructions, 41
Brown, Charlie, 97
Building Leadership Teams, viii
Buzz Group, The, 30–31

Card Discovery Problem, 62–63
Carroll, John S., 4
Charrette Planning Process, 166
Checklists, 76
Cleveland, Grover, 69
Coercing Agreement, 145
collaborative teaming, 3
Collegiality
    Assessment, 21–22
    inventory, 22–23
Committee Hearing, The, 90
complacency, 5
Conflict
    and Cooperation, 149
    interference in decision making, 140

    resolution,
        defined, 139
        essential attitudes for, 140–141
consensus
    as leadership skill, 3
    Brainstorming, 125
    decision making
        advantages, 115–116
        guidelines/ground rules, 114–115
        ranking, 116
        voting, 116
    defined, 3, 113
Cooperative Groups, 84–85
creativity
    defined, 65–66
    inhibited, 66

de Bono, Edward, 66
decision making
    quality, 4, 10
    shared, 3, 5, 6
        pitfalls, 11, 12
        reasons for, 5
    team, 6
decision-making methods, 1–3
    by authority after group discussion, 2
    by authority after no group discussion, 2
    by averaging individuals' opinions, 2
    by clique, 2
    by consensus, 3
    by default, 2
    by expert, 2
    by majority vote, 3
    by minority, 3
    self-authorized, 2
decision-making process, basic stages, 4
decisions
    bad, 4, 5
    team 6, 7
Delbecq, Andre L., 154
Delphi Process, 155–157
Dialogue, The, 91
Diamonds Nine, 129
Display, 130
Discussion, 66, 122
Doyle, Michael, 9, 10
DuBois, Rachel, 140
Duell, Charles H., 69

Ecclesiastes, 6
educational reform, 3, 5
effective team roles, 35
effective work group, 8

Einstein, Albert, 66, 95
Fault Tree Analysis, 75
Fayol, Henri, 155
Filley, Alan C., 140
Fishbone Diagram, 105–106
Fishbowl Strategy, 144
Fist-to-Five, 133–134
Flowcharts, 168–169
Force Field Analysis, 100–101
    worksheet, 102
Forest, Marcia, 163
Francis, Dave, 37
Franklin, Benjamin, 81

Gallery, The, 85–86
Game of Chicken, The, 141–143
    scoring sheet, 143
Generating Ideas, process activities for, 68–80
    Brainstorming, 68–70
    Checklists, 76
    Fault Tree Analysis, 75
    Ideawriting, 78–79
    Kiva Technique, 79–80
    Mind Mapping, 73–75
    Nominal Group Technique, 70–72
Goal Setting and Planning, process activities for, 155–172
    Action Logs, 169–170
    Charrette Planning Process, 166
    Delphi Process, 155–157
    Flowcharts, 168–169
    Group Goal Setting, 157–158
    How?-By Pursuit, 161–162
    Mixed Scanning Strategy, 167–168
    Modified MAPS, 163–165
    Nominal Group Technique, 158–161
    Path, The, 171–172
good team, characteristics of, 7, 8
Group Conversation, 150–151
Group Goal Setting, 157–158
group memory, 10
group process, 10, 11
Gordon, Thomas, 5
Guess Who?, 32
Gustafson, David H., 154

Helmer, O., 10
Hollow Square
    key, 52
    observing team briefing sheet, 51
    operating team briefing sheet, 49
    pattern, 53
    planning team briefing sheet, 50
How?-By Pursuit, 161–162
    Diagram, 162
Huddle Method, The, 122

Ideawriting, 78–79
If My School Were . . ., 15–16
Individual and Group Assessment Collaborative
    Skills, 54–56
    checklist, 55–56
    information
    defined, 81
    determining accuracy and sufficiency, 82–83
    forms of, 81
Interrogation Panel, The, 88–89
Interview, The, 92
Ishikawa Diagram, 105–106

Janis, Irving L., 12
Johnson, David W., 1, 114
Johnson, Eric J., 4
Johnson, Frank P., 1, 114

Kepner, Charles H., 82
King, Matthew, 14
Kiva Technique, The, 79–80

leadership skills, 3
*Leading Your Team to Excellence,* goals of, ix
Lecture, The, 93–94
Lewin, Kurt, 100
Li, Mew–Soong, 140
Lost on the Moon, 42–47
    consensus instructions, 45
    instructions, 44
    NASA rankings, 46
    scoring sheet, 47
Lynch, Robert F., 15, 34, 115

Making a Set of Squares, directions for, 40
MAPS
    Modified, 163–165
    Questions, The, 164
    Sample, 165
McGregor, Douglas, 8
meeting, good
    conducting, 9
    eighteen steps for, 9
Mencken, H. L., 96
Milliken, Robert, 67
Mind Mapping, 73–74
mission statements, 120, 121
Mixed Scanning Strategy, 167–168
Montaigne, 154
Multivoting, 131

Name Tag Mixer, 19–20
    sample, 20
Nominal Group Technique, 70–72, 98–100, 158–161

Osborn Checklist, 79

Panel Discussion, The, 89–90
Parker, Glenn M., 34
Parking Lot Meetings, 128
participatory management, 3
Path, The, 171–72
Path Process Sample Diagram, 171, 173
Phillips 66, 122
planning, successful, 154
Priority Matrix, 135–138
    samples, 136, 137
Prisoner's Dilemma, 146–148
    Scoring Instructions, 148
    Tally Sheet, 148

problem solvers, characteristics of, 97
problem solving
    process activities for, 98–102
        Affinity Process, 103–104
        Fishbone Diagram, 105–106
        Force Field Analysis, 100–101
        Ishikawa Diagram, 105–106
        Nominal Group Technique, 98–100
        Situation–Target–Proposal, 110–112
        Why?–Because Pursuit, 108–110
        WOTS Up Analysis, 106–107
    seven steps, 97
problems
    avoidance of, 95
    categories of, 96–97
    characteristics of, 96
    structures of, 96
process activities, steps in, 15
process expert, functions of, 10
procrastination, 5

Ranking, 127–28
Reducing Conflict, process activities for, 141–152
    Air Time, 151–152
    Coercing Agreement, 145
    Conflict and Cooperation, 149
    Fishbowl Strategy, 144
    Game of Chicken, The, 141–143
    Group Conversation, 150–151
    Prisoner's Dilemma, 146–148
    Walking a Mile in the Other's Moccasins, 152
Role Playing, 28–29
Roosevelt, Teddy, 153

Saphier, Jon, 14
Scanning Strategy, 132
school culture
    assessment, 24–28
    inventory, norms of, 26–28
    twelve norms of, 26
Sharing Critical Information, process activities for, 84–94
    Committee Hearing, The, 90
    Cooperative Groups, 84–85
    Dialogue, The, 91
    Gallery, The, 85–86
    Interrogation Panel, The, 88–89
    Interview, The, 92
    Lecture, The, 93–94
    Panel Discussion, The, 87–88
    Symposium, The, 86–87
Simon, Virginia, 7
Situation–Target–Proposal, 110–112
    worksheet, 111
Sloma, Richard S., 153, 154
Small Group Discussion, 29–30
Snow, Judith, 163
Speaker, Tris, 65
Spend-a-Buck, 134–135
Stengel, Casey, 3
Straus, David, 9, 10
Symposium, The, 86–87
Szent–Gyorgi, Albert, 65

team building, 33–35
    process activities for, 38–66
        Are We Really a Team?, 55–58
        Assessment of Collaboration Skills, 53–55
        Broken Squares, 38–41
        Card Discovery Problem, 62–63
        Hollow Square Pattern, 48–53
        Lost on the Moon, 42–47
        Team Development Scale, 60–62
team development
    key factors needed, 35
    scale, 60–62
        checklist, 62–63
    stages of, 34
team players, types of, 35–36
team progress, areas of assessment for, 33–34
team trouble, warning signals, 37
Townsend, Robert, 2
Tregoe, Benjamin B., 82
Two Truths and a Lie, 17–18
Turkey Trot, 31–32

values and decision–making process, 14
    building and sharing, process activities for, 15–32
        Buzz Group, The, 31–32
        Collegiality Assessment, 21–22
        Guess Who?, 32
        If My School Were . . . , 15–16
        Name Tag Mixer, 19–20
        Role Playing, 29–30
        School Culture Assessment, 24–28
        Small Group Discussion, 30–31
        Turkey Trot, 31–32
        Two Truths and a Lie, 17–18
        Wanted . . . for, 18–19
        What's in Your Wallet?, 16–17
    defined, 14
    phases of development, 14
    in team building, 14
Van de Ven, Andrew H., 154
Vigilant Analysis, 123

Walking a Mile in the Other's Moccasins, 152
Wanted . . . for, 18–19
Werner, Thomas J., 15, 34, 115
What's in Your Wallet?, 16–17
Wheeler, Daniel D., 12
Whitman, Walt, 141
Why?–Because Pursuit, 108
    diagram, 109
WOTS Up Analysis, 106–107
    planning form, 107

Young, Don, 37

In compliance with GPSR, should you have any concerns about the safety of this product, please advise: International Associates Auditing & Certification Limited The Black Church, St Mary's Place, Dublin 7, D07 P4AX Ireland EUAR@ie.ia-net.com

www.ingramcontent.com/pod-product-compliance
Lightning Source LLC
Chambersburg PA
CBHW051210290426
44109CB00021B/2407